When Saints Are Lovers

The Spirituality of Maryknoll Co-Founder Thomas F. Price

John T. Seddon III

Foreword
by
William D. McCarthy, M.M.

A Liturgical Press Book

THE LITURGICAL PRESS
Collegeville, Minnesota

Cover design by David Manahan, O.S.B. Photo Courtesy of Maryknoll Missioners.

Grateful acknowledgement is made to the Maryknoll Archives, Maryknoll, New York, for permission to use the Reverend Thomas Frederick Price, M.M., material, especially his *Diary*, and to the University of Notre Dame Archives, South Bend, Indiana, for permission to use material concerning T. F. Price from *The Society of the Propagation of the Faith Material*.

1   2   3   4   5   6   7   8

Library of Congress Cataloging-in-Publication Data

Seddon, John T., 1945–
    When saints are lovers : the spirituality of Maryknoll co-founder
Thomas F. Price / John T. Seddon III.
        p.   cm.
    Includes bibliographical references.
    ISBN 0-8146-2228-3
    1. Price, Thomas Frederick, 1860–1919. 2. Bernadette,
Saint, 1844–1879—Cult. 3. Price, Thomas Frederick, 1860–1919—
Diaries. 4. Catholic Foreign Mission Society of America—
Biography.   I. Title.
BX4705.P7S43   1997
271'.79—dc21
[B]   97-1793
                                                         CIP

Contents

Foreword

John Seddon has written the first study in depth of the mystical journey that was at the heart of the missionary spirituality of Maryknoll's senior cofounder, Fr. Thomas Frederick Price.

It was Father Price who led the first group of four Maryknoll priests to Kongmoon in southern China in 1918. At that time he was himself already an experienced evangelizer, having spent twenty-five years traveling throughout his native North Carolina ministering to widely dispersed small Catholic communities and struggling to make appealing presentations of Catholicism to the state's much more numerous Protestant population. He had established a center for the training of priests for the North Carolina Apostolate as he named it. He had founded an orphanage. He had also put his missionary zeal into *Truth*, his own national magazine in which he sought to provide accurate information about the Catholic faith for readers of all confessions. Soon his vision expanded to embrace missions overseas, a perspective he had heard forcefully expressed in 1904 by the young director of the Society for the Propagation of the Faith of the Archdiocese of Boston Fr. James Anthony Walsh. In 1910 Price proposed that the two immediately combine their efforts to found for the church in the United States a foreign mission society and seminary. Walsh readily accepted the challenge, and Father Price secured the support of his former pastor and now the leading United States Catholic churchman, James Cardinal Gibbons of Baltimore. The leadership of Gibbons facilitated the unanimous endorsement of the project by the archbishops at their annual meeting in 1911. Price and Walsh brought the authorization to Rome, and canonical establishment was promptly granted by Pope Pius X. Maryknoll, formally The Catholic Foreign Mission Society of America, was born. Price's initiative had been indispensable in bringing to reality the dream both founders shared.

Father Price would be with Father Walsh and the young society just eight more years. He died of acute appendicitis in Hong Kong in 1919 just months after opening Maryknoll's first mission in Yeungkong in south China. He was fifty-nine.

These eight years were not easy ones for Father Price. While Father Walsh directed the new seminary and society, and edited its magazine, the *Field Afar,* Father Price, drawing on his experience as a traveling preacher and fund raiser, journeyed around the country making Maryknoll known in parishes and begging for its support. He did this with great personal sacrifice. Many times the work was more of an ordeal for him than others realized. Much more congenial for him was the occasional role as a spiritual director whenever he was back at the seminary.

In addition to the difficulty inherent in constant traveling and begging, Father Price was experiencing at this time two deep challenges in his life. One concerned the direction of the new society. Father Price thought that it should send missioners not only to non-Christian lands but to other areas where priests were too few to meet pastoral needs such as the Philippines, Latin America, and the southern United States. This was not the view of Father Walsh. Maryknoll had been approved by Rome as a society committed to work among "heathens." In 1914 and again in 1916 Father Price seriously considered withdrawing from Maryknoll to create a new organization with a broader scope. Though he ultimately remained in the society, this issue continued to be a source of painful inner conflict for him.

But there was another challenge that was deeply affecting Father Price at this time, and is the principal subject of this book. His spirituality was drawing him in a profoundly mystical direction.

This development broke in upon him in 1911 while he was still in Europe after his visit to Rome with Father Walsh. So intense was this experience that, as he wrote privately, it "changed my whole life." Even the mission project would "no longer absorb" him but would be "subordinate" to living the "new life" that he sensed was enfolding him. This new life was experienced in the form of profoundly close spiritual relationships. He had long been seeking closer union with Christ, and he had long had an ever-deepening affection for the Virgin Mary to whom he had been writing daily letters since 1908. Now, however, in the course of a visit to the great Marian shrine at Lourdes he had found in the saintly (though not yet canonized) Bernadette Soubirous (1844–1879) an extraordinary patron. He would soon regard her as his "dear sister," and then his "spouse." Since she had been so loved by Mary as to have been privileged with eighteen apparitions and to have heard from the Virgin's lips her title of the Immaculate Conception, Bernadette seemed the perfect friend to link Father Price to their common mother and to Jesus. So real were these bonds for him that he bought a silver ring and had it engraved with emblems and dates of the stages in the unfolding of these intimate relationships. Explaining the ring in a confidential letter to the cardinal prefect of the Congregation for the Propagation of the Faith in Rome, he wrote, "For some years my soul has been in a state of special inseparable and constant Divine union, the seal of which is in the wearing of this ring." As a final testimony of his tender love of Bernadette, he left the written request that after his death his heart be interred in the crypt near her body at the convent of the Sisters of Charity of Christian Instruction in Nevers, France. It rests there today.

While this new experience was an enormous support for Price, it occasioned some misunderstandings in his relationship with Father Walsh. Walsh was himself a man of serious prayer and urged that every Maryknoller be "a contemplative in action." Nevertheless, as Father Price's "devotions" increased and multiplied, it became unpredictable when his practical services could be engaged. Though Father Walsh clearly sensed that his cofounder was a deeply spiritual man, Father Price did not disclose to him or other Maryknoll colleagues the experience that was stealing his heart—and his time. Understandably, he shared his secret only with his spiritual directors, a Sulpician, and later a Jesuit. Father Walsh came to refer to Father Price as the "Mary" of Maryknoll while he was himself resigned to the role of "Martha."

Father Price finished his life faithful to the society he had helped establish. He enjoined the French priest who was with him as he lay dying to "tell Father Walsh my last thoughts were for them all, and that I died in the love of Jesus, Mary, Joseph, and of Maryknoll." Father Walsh later always referred to Father Price with affection and terms of reverence such as "my sainted co-founder" or "the saintly Fr. Price." And so has he always been remembered by Maryknollers.

The privileged historical source for an exploration of the spirituality of Father Price is the collection of his 3,087 daily diary-like letters written between 1908 and his death in 1919. Though he marked the notebooks containing the letters as "strictly private," he did preserve them and did not destroy them when illness began to threaten his life. The late Fr. John McConnell who was the final editor of their transcription stated that it could only be concluded that Father Price intended that they be preserved and so eventually read by others.

Dr. Seddon has thoroughly studied these letters along with other documents concerning Father Price. Though Maryknoller Fr. John C. Murrett used these materials in writing his popular biography of Father Price (*Tar Heel Apostle* [1944]), Seddon is the first scholar to attempt an analysis of the mystical depth discernible in Price's unique spirituality. What is the nature of these deep relationships he experienced? How is one to interpret the special role of Bernadette Soubirous in his journey? And are there parallels in the lives of other Christian saints or mystics? These were questions that Father Price himself seems sometimes to have asked.

Dr. Seddon's insightful work enables us to penetrate more fully this unusual circumstance when saints are indeed lovers.

William D. McCarthy, M.M.

Preface

Dealing with Thomas Frederick Price has proven to be both a challenging study and a fascinating journey. One of the most exciting aspects of this study was the construction of a critical method for analyzing a spiritual journey in a cross-cultural environment. At first glance, this project might seem to be a study of a celibate's piety, but, in actuality, it is about the impact of culture on theology and spirituality in general and, most importantly, it yields insights into married spirituality.

This project was unknowingly begun by William McCarthy, M.M., who, as friend and then professor of history at the Maryknoll School of Theology, was sharing Price's story over dinner at our home. Bill mentioned that Robert Sheridan, M.M., was completing the publication of the over three thousand personal daily letters that Price had written to the Blessed Mother. Our dinner guest also spoke of Price's struggles, ordination, wedding ring, and relationship to Bernadette of Lourdes. After being "introduced" to Price and Bernadette at dinner, I could not get them or the transcribed letters out of my mind.

Shortly after that I met with Bob Sheridan and explained the critical approach I wanted to take in studying Price's spirituality. Bob was very supportive and during the following years insured that I have all the information available. Since that time the Maryknoll Fathers archivists have been extremely cooperative and supportive and the Maryknoll librarians, James O'Halloran and the late Arthur Brown, were of tremendous assistance.

In addition to the Maryknollers, I wish to express many thanks to several gentlemen at Fordham University: Richard

Smith, S.J., then chair of the theology department, early on recognized the importance of Fred Price's spirituality and encouraged my continuing work. Professor John J. Heaney's insights into religion and psychology were very helpful. Professor Ewert H. Cousins' support and critical method work were very instrumental in helping me to understand Price. To all of these gentlemen a special thanks for their understanding and acceptance of my dyslexia. Additional methodological insights and encouragement were provided by Asher Finkel, chair of the Jewish-Christian Graduate Program at Seton Hall.

Other people who supported my studies and research included the members of the Marriage Encounter Region in Stamford back in the 1970s, the 105 MAG, 137 MAG, and Hq NYANG. A special thanks to Bill Anderson for his technical documentation support.

Most importantly, without the support of my loving family, this could not have been done. Without Tom and Eric who understood that "Dad is working" and my wife Anne's encouragement, theological sharing, and editing of the "final drafts" of the dissertation, this study would still be a proposal or a manuscript.

Finally, I thank you, the reader, who at the end of this project's journey will hopefully gain new insight and a desire to share your own personal journey with others.

The text is arranged in such a way that the reader may either directly begin the story of Fred Price's spiritual journey with chapter 1, 2, 3, etc. . . . or, for those interested in methodology, after chapter 1 read appendixes A and B. Either way, appendix C (Chronology) is recommended as a helpful guide.

John T. Seddon III

1

A Unique Marriage

This is a study of a unique marriage. The groom, born at the beginning of the American Civil War in 1860, was a southern gentleman, "Mr. North Carolina" according to his friends, later, he became a major figure in the American Roman Catholic missionary movement. He died on mission in Hong Kong, China, in September 1919.

The bride was a poor, sickly girl from a rural mountain village in southern France. As a teenager she had visions of the Blessed Mother in 1858. Later she became a Sister of Charity and Christian Instruction and spent a quiet life of humble service at the motherhouse of the Order in Nevers, France. Upon her death in 1879, she was buried in the crypt below the convent's chapel. She was recognized as a saint by Rome in 1933.

The couple did not meet until 1911, or thirty-two years after the bride's death. Their romance, courtship, and marriage is recorded in the groom's *Diary*. Through his *Diary* we have a window into the life of this extraordinary couple and their private relationship with God.

Welcome to the study of the dynamic spiritual life of Fr. Thomas Frederick Price, M.M., who gives us an example of married love as a way of prayer and seeking union with God. Together, Fred Price (as he was known to his friends) and his bride, Bernadette Soubirous of Lourdes, call us to look at the serious effect of culture on our own spiritual journey and for us to reevaluate the meaning of the phrase "married in Christ."

In this study, we will explore the cultural and spiritual foundations of Fred Price's life and see how they developed into a dedication to the Blessed Mother and romantic relationship with Bernadette. While she is well known and recognized as a famous mystic, he is not very familiar to many people outside the circles of those concerned with the American missionary movement. Fred was a unique and colorful character in the American Roman Catholic Church and a leader in American Roman Catholic missionary movement.

Born in Wilmington, North Carolina, in 1860, Fred Price emerges out of a southern American post-Civil War culture to become one of the most important leaders of the American Roman Catholic missionary effort in the late nineteenth and early twentieth centuries. Along with being the co-founder of the first Roman Catholic foreign mission society and seminary in the United States, Maryknoll (officially, the Catholic Foreign Mission Society of America), Fred led Maryknoll's first missionary band which deployed to China. Prior to his Maryknoll efforts he is known for being the first native North Carolinian ordained as a Roman Catholic diocesan priest. Furthermore, he founded the North Carolina Apostolic Company, a home mission society, which in addition to its mission center had an orphanage and school. During that time, he was the founder and editor of *Truth* and *Orphan Boy* magazines. Later Fred also edited two English-language biographies on Bernadette Soubirous of Lourdes.

Our Sources for the Study

Without a doubt Fred Price's most significant contribution to Christian life is his rich and complex spiritual life which he recorded in over three thousand daily letters to the Blessed Mother during the last eleven years of his life. These letters are called Father Price's *Diary* by the Maryknoll Community. It is the *Diary* that reveals his relationship with the Blessed Mother and his intimate life with Bernadette and the Holy Trinity.

This study is the first on Fred Price that focuses on the *Diary* and the relationship between Fred and Bernadette. During his life many people recognized that Fred had a special relationship with Bernadette. Shortly after Fred Price's death in 1919,

Fr. James Edward Walsh, M.M., came across thirty-four hand-written notebooks containing the *Diary* at the first Maryknoll mission center in Yeungkong, China. He immediately realized that it was a "very special document" and shipped it back to the United States from China. Two factors stand out as to why this special relationship between Fred and Bernadette has not been explored sooner: the deep personal nature of the relationhip revealed in the *Diary* and the great difficulty in transcribing its 3,087 letters.

While Fred Price has left us an extensive amount of his own writings and edited works, we also have the writings of others that consist of three biographies, one of which is the well-known *Tarheel Apostle,** a book entitled *The Spiritual Legacy of the Co-Founders,*** Robert Sheridan's *The Founders of Maryknoll,* and a chapter or brief mention about Father Price in the histories of the Society. Additionally, the Maryknoll Fathers and Brothers held a symposium concerning Fred Price in 1956, which resulted in a collection of testimonies about him and places and events in his life. This was updated by Fr. Robert E. Sheridan, M.M., in 1981. These secondary sources provide excellent background material for understanding the general flow of Father Price's life.***

Our Route to Discovering the Marriage

This study will look into the private life of Fred Price. Through that experience we will look into the core of human life or the experience of the ultimate transcendence where the human encounters the divine.

The objective of this case study in spirituality is *not* to write a biography, *nor* to collect a systematic theological position, *nor* to

---

*The first biography entitled *Father Price of Maryknoll* was written by Patrick J. Byrne in 1923. An unpublished manuscript was completed by George C. Powers in 1943, and the well-known biography by John C. Murrett, *Tarheel Apostle,* was published in 1944.

**This book is a collection of notes on religious practices and virtues from the biographies. Its descriptions ignore spirituality and the spiritual journey.

***All of the sources concerning Father Price to be used in this study are discussed in appendix B.

list devotional practices, *nor* is it a study written for the purpose
of instructing others how to live a holy life. Rather it is an attempt
to discover the deepest center of an individual's being, the point
of which one is open to the transcendent. In this study we will
analyze the dynamics of an individual's development and the
journey towards the goal of union with the divine.

The relationships stated by Fred Price in his writings are so
special, unique, and important that they demand that we use a
strict critical method to insure a proper understanding of the
statements, events surrounding the relationships and situations
and the accurate evaluation of the relationship (no less critical
than those of the Quest for the Historical Jesus).

When we are working with a person's spirituality, we are
dealing with the very personal dynamics of an individual. We
could back away from the challenge of carefully analyzing the
story related to us in various sources, but the story is so special
and at first glance unique that it deserves a greater effort on our
part to understand what really happened during the spiritual
journey. This means going beyond just the historical facts, the
cultural analysis, the philosophical rationalization,[1] or the psychological reflections on the situation. This means looking beyond an analysis of the doctrinal statements of the individual(s)
one is studying. We need to look at the experiences that involve
and affect the total person. We need to focus on the personal dis-
covery made at the core of one's being, a person's spiritual depth.
Specifically, in studying spirituality we are looking at the deepest
center of the human that is open to the transcendent dimension.[2]

In working with another person's spirituality, one begins to
grow in the awareness that we are not dealing with something
that is the "other worldly," "non-being," or "non-physical" but
rather something that involves a person's total being and their relationship with the ultimate reality. It is important that a person's
spirituality not be understood in the dualistic body and soul context but rather that the person be seen as the totality of body, soul,
mind, spirit, psyche, and strength.

In analyzing a spirituality and the experience of the ultimate
transcendent, we are dealing with the oldest area of human
study and also the newest academic discipline.[3] We shall use the

multi-disciplinary tools of this discipline with its specific techniques for analyzing the spiritual journey and critically* evaluating a spiritual experience.

This approach will enable us not only to get to the root of a spirituality, its unique experience, but to evaluate the experience. It also provides a means of accurately describing the situations and theologies being studied, enables us to compare the spiritual experience to other experiences and to systematic theologies, and establishes criteria to evaluate the spiritual experience(s).

Our method of analysis has THREE PHASES with SEVEN STEPS. The First Phase, Discovering, begins with STEP ONE looking at the sources available to us and the Cultural Setting(s) of our groom and his bride. STEP TWO starts by seeking the foundations that the groom's spiritual journey is built upon and then looks at his spiritual journey and experiences. The Second Phase is concerned with Extracting Fred Price's expressive or systematic theology (STEP THREE) and the Experiential Theology or Spirituality (STEP FOUR). Phase Three, Evaluating, has three steps and uses comparisons to fully understand the implications of the spirituality. In the first of these comparisons, STEP FIVE, the Expressed and Experienced Theologies are placed side by side. Next STEP SIX looks at the spirituality of this study and the phenomenon of transcendence. Finally, in STEP SEVEN, our groom's experience is compared to the spiritual tradition that most closely matches his experience, the Judeo-Christian "Canticle" or "Love" Tradition. Some readers may desire a more detailed presentation of the method and criteria used in this study. This is provided in appendix A. The chart on the next page gives an overview of the three phases, seven steps, and chapters of this book.

In Thomas Frederick Price we are dealing with a man who is "bigger than one issue" and multi-talented. His theology is important because it is the springboard for his spirituality which in turn propels his missionary zeal. We are dealing with a person of

*"Critical" in this context does not mean being negative towards something; rather it means being rigorous in looking at it, applying universal criteria of judgment and analytical methods that will lead to objective conclusions.

considerable spiritual depth, creative ideas, and unwavering dedication. Most of the issues he deals with are lifelong and are therefore interwoven throughout his journey.

```
                        FIGURE #1
                   CHAPTER SUMMARY
Phase STEP                                      Chapter
I. DISCOVERING
     STEP 1 The Sources and Setting
               1a The Source                    1 (apdx.B)
               1b The Cultural Setting           2
     STEP 2 Journey and Experience
               2a The Foundations               3, 4, 5, 6*
               2b The Development               9, 10
II.  EXTRACTING
     STEP 3 The Expressive Theology             7, 8
     STEP 4 The Experiential Theology           11
III. EVALUATING
     STEP 5 Theological Comparison              12
     STEP 6 Transcendent Evaluation             13
     STEP 7 Setting In the Tradition            14
CONCLUSIONS                                     15
```

*The next chapter does not follow in sequence. This is unique to studying Thomas Frederick Price, who did most of his systematic (expressional theological) writings before 1912, during step 2a. Therefore, to give the reader a better feel for his life journey, the expressive theology is discussed (chapters 8 and 9) before the spiritual experiences are investigated (chapters 10 and 11).

Notes

   1. For a discussion of getting beyond the skepticism of the modern era scientific empiricism, see Jonathan Shear, "On Mystical Experiences as Support for the Perennial Philosophy," *Journal of the American Academy of Religion* 62:2 (Summer 1994) 319–42.
   2. Ewert H. Cousins, "Preface to the Series," "World Spirituality" Series, *Christian Spirituality, Post-Reformation and Modern* (New York: Crossroad, 1989) xii.
   3. For a discussion of spirituality as an academic discipline, see: Bradley C. Hanson, ed., *Modern Christian Spirituality* (Atlanta: Scholars, 1990); Ewert H. Cousins, "Preface to the Series" [World Spirituality: An Encyclopedic History of the Religious Quest] in *Christian Spirituality II,* Bernard McGinn, John Meyendorff, and Jean Leclercq, eds. (New York: Crossroad, 1986) xii; Sandra Schneiders, "Theology and Spirituality: Strangers, Rivals, or Partners?" *Horizons* 13:2 (1955) 253–74; Bernard McGinn, "The Letter and the Spirit: Spirituality as an Academic Discipline," *Christian Spirituality Bulletin* 1:2 (Fall 1993) 1–10.

2

Cultural and Spiritual Setting

The link between culture and spiritual journey is interesting, in fact vital, to understanding not only people from the past but our own spiritual journeys and experiences. In order to understand we must care enough about those we are studying to, as the ancient American saying goes, sincerely "walk a mile in their moccasins." This begins with the study of their culture.

Our Times and Theirs

We cannot begin to understand the writing let alone the experiences of another if we lack the courage to step into their time, their space, their view of the world. Certainly in the case of Thomas Frederick Price and Bernadette Soubirous to fail to accept their culture would lead to our failure to truly understand them.

When we come in contact with a culture that is not our own either through travel or, as in this case, intense study we can experience *cultural shock*. Our reactions can range from *going native* (total acceptance of the new culture and rejection of our old one) to *flight* or *fight* (total rejection of the new cultural experience and stating that our own is the only correct one) or anything in between. We must be flexible in accepting judgments. Only then can we achieve an accurate description that can be objectively analyzed and critically reviewed.

The same is true if we are not familiar with the type of spiritual tradition, which in the case of this paper is the "canticle" or "love" tradition, we can experience *spirituality shock*. For those of us not immersed in the courtly love tradition of the South or familiar with the Christian canticle tradition, the journey to understanding Fred Price's experience may prove to be a very rewarding experience.

It is obvious that there are significant differences in the physical surroundings between Fred Price's world and our world today. Electricity, automobiles and super highways, and airplanes were only emerging during Fred Price's lifetime. What is not quite as obvious but far more important to this study is that the issues for society and the Church were different as well. The Roman Catholic Church was coping with Modernism and its threat to the faith.[1] Today we are struggling with the issues of "birth control" and liberation theology.[2] Present-day methods of biblical exegesis and systematic theology were not part of Fred Price's experience. In order to understand Fred Price, it is imperative to start where he starts: immersed in their culture.

Southern Culture

The South as a regional culture has fascinated southerners and non-southerners alike. It is a dynamic society with its chivalry and honor that dominated from pre-slave times to the present. It is a culture that prided itself on gallantry, politeness, and the charm of chivalry.[3]

While the popular concept of southern culture is the high society of the plantation life-style of the anti-bellum period, it would be incorrect to view this part of the South as different or separate from the rest of society. The southern culture we are dealing with is not just the slave-holding planter society, nor are we solely dealing with a pro-slavery society in general but rather the broader southern society that included urbanites, yeomen farmers, the poor, slaves, and professionals that had a common cultural base.

Key characteristics of southern society include a sense of place, interest in the concrete with time moving slower than in the North, and importance of the present moment, a sense of history, and community, i.e., the individual in the family with its place in the community,[4] plus the Cavalier background of the society from its beginnings in 1607. These contributed the overwhelming importance of chivalry and its code of honor in society.

The entire society well before the Revolutionary War* had already been permeated with the values of chivalry and the courtly love tradition, with its specific relationships between the sexes and its concepts of honor and its social structure and geographic place.

The strong tradition of southern chivalry and courtly love was celebrated as courtly love in novels. Many of these books became "the inspiration for such extravaganzas as the *opèra bouffe* title of "the chivalry" by which the ruling class . . . . habitually designated itself."[5] A gallant, proper, polite, and charming gentleman was what was expected of the southern male and all reports indicate that Fred Price was a charming southern gentleman.[6]

Part of the breeding of a southern gentleman was a classical education. The Greek and Latin classics were the ideal societies which were reference points for southern society and the concept of primal honor.[7] Fred Price received such an education at St. Charles College and St. Mary's Seminary in Baltimore.

This tradition in the South was heir to the chivalrous tradition of the Middle Ages with its courtly love and images of the knight riding off on a quest for the *honor* of the lady of the castle. This cultural milieu was the context for Father Price's developing a personal spirituality which we shall see involved devotion to the Blessed Mother and Bernadette Soubirous.

Honor

The chivalry society was maintained by the concept of honor. Honor determined social rank. It was the moral code. It was through honor that "self-worth, gentility, and high-mindedness,

---

*In pre-Revolutionary New England and southern colonial times, the cultures were not as far apart as they were in the Civil War era. However, today the Yankees among us need to enter into this different society in order to understand Fred Price and to a large extent the very similar French culture into which Bernadette Soubirous was born. It may sound fanciful to the non-southern ear, but it was sincerely meant and felt by the southerners who lived within the cultural context.

or public repute, valor for family and country [south], and conformity to community wishes."[8] At the heart of honor, then, lies public evaluation.[9] Honor literally became a god. It was the cornerstone of the society:

> The chief aim of this notion of honor was to protect the individual, group, or race from the greatest dread that its adherents could imagine. That fear was not death, dying with honor would bring glory. Rather, the fear was of public humiliation.[10]

Honor insured social bonding and a place within the community. Honor then is what secures one's (the family's) place in society. It is the "how" that goes with the "what" of the sacred duty that one would vow to uphold.

For women honor is much more socially controlled than a man's. She cannot act shamelessly and yet retain respect.[11] For both sexes the private and the public were indistinguishable, as was the individual and the family as well.[12]

The concept of primal honor reached to the heart of southern society. Honor is everything and it is not an abstraction or ideal but rather an inter-personal reality. It is necessary for a place in society. What is important is that others perceive the individual and his/her family as honest, rather than some objective criteria of honest action.[13]

Honor was individually acted upon but not individually reflected. This honor was group honor, or more specifically family honor, and in that context guaranteed a place in society. Private family life was public, with no dichotomy between the two.[14]

Physical and social place were critical to southerners and were also intertwined. Individuals and their families identified themselves with a place regardless of social standing. John Dabbs has pointed out that the plantation owner and his family belonged to the place as much as the slaves.[15] Being separated from the place physically or by loss of honor was a terrible thing.

It is difficult to express the overwhelming fear of loneliness that came with loss of place or rather honor. Loss of honor was much broader than financial problems causing loss of social status. In fact, no matter how poor one was one could have honor.

In the context of chivalry and honor, four critical elements of southern conduct emerge:

1) honor as immortalizing valor,
2) the opinion of others is a key part of personal identity,
3) physical appearance as a sign of inner merit,
4) the defense of male integrity is critical and coupled with a mingled fear and love of women.[16]

Southern Women

Southern women were held in a place of honor by their gallant, noble gentlemen. These women were the brides and wives who were so important in carrying on the society.[17] The exalted position of southern women resembled the courtly love traditions of the lady of the castle, in which the man defended her and in the process received meaning and purpose. In southern society the lady of the castle was the wife, not some lady off afar or an ideal.

Yankee attacks on the sexual mores of southern society resulted in women being glorified:

> The upshot, in this land of spreading notions of chivalry, was downright gyneolatry. She was the South's Palladium, this Southern woman—the shield-bearing Athena gleaming whitely in the clouds, the standard for its rallying, the mystic symbol of its nationality in face of the foe. . . . There was . . . hardly a brave speech that did not open and close with the clash of shields and the flourishing of swords for her glory.
>
> "Women! ! ! the center and circumference, diameter and periphery, sine, tangent and secant of all our affections!" Such was the toast which brought twenty great cheers from the audience at the celebration of Georgia's one-hundredth anniversary in 1830.[18]

Idealized but circumscribed, the southern wife learned to dominate the home and family with great authority, while in public life her husband dealt with the other males. It was a patriarchal society with a rejection of the "arguments for the equality of the sexes within marriage." The ideal southern woman was not only ethereal but also hardworking, politically aware (though never mingled in discussion), and prudent in household management.[19] Southern women were managers of the house but would not conduct business outside of the home. Even if the women owned property, the sale would be negotiated by her husband, male relative, or an attorney (also male).

The southern mother was called "the kinkeeper" and was responsible for the bravery and honor of the family.[20] A person's honor not only reflected upon the individual but also the family and especially the kinkeeper. The kinkeeper position had the tremendous moral power of the mother and was important to women due to their limited public life and power in society.[21]

Over the centuries the courtly love had become intertwined with the marital love tradition. A reciprocal loving, conjugal union was the norm for marriage by the twelfth century during the emergence of the courtly love tradition.[22] Though the tradition often sang of adultery,[23] these relationships, such as Lancelot and Guinevere, just as often ended in disaster for all and was an important lesson for the reader on the results of such acts. However, the romance that courtly love brought to male-female relationships was not restricted to adulterous relationships in real life.[24]

The tradition of married reciprocal and faithful love is found in the twelfth-century monastic spiritual love tradition which is expressed in sensual courtly love literary forms.[25] A twelfth-century treatise on courtly love suggests a strong link between courtly love and marriage.[26] In the fourteenth century secular writings seem to integrate courtly and married love.[27] By the sixteenth century there is a popular integration of the two.[28]

It is important to realize that this courtly love cultural root developed in France, England, Spain, and Italy and that not only was Fred immersed in this cultural milieu but so was Bernadette.

Spiritual Love Tradition and Culture

Fred Price's spiritual experience was shaped by the southern culture as much as by doctrinal teaching and devotional exercises. Southern society in the nineteenth century as an American remnant of the European courtly society that emerged in the Middle Ages forms a cultural link with the great religious Orders that emerged during the twelfth and thirteenth centuries in France and Italy and the sixteenth century in Spain.

These Orders used the secular understanding of chivalry, the love of a man for a woman, as a foundation for their spirituality. They drew from the Canticles tradition, Judaism and Christianity, and their culture. In the twelfth century Bernard of Clairvaux described the mystical union of the soul with Christ to his fellow Cistercians, using the powerful sensual male-female love images that flowered within society at that time. This mystical tradition is continued by Francis of Assisi who emerges from the knightly tradition of Italian courtly love in the thirteenth century. He seeks his beloved Lady Poverty as a knight seeking the lady of the castle. Fred Price's spiritual experience is a continuation of the beautiful loving union that emerged in the Middle Ages. As the study of Fred's life unfolds, we will see the social concepts of chivalry and the need for an inter-personal life mix with the individualistic Counter-Reformation Church teaching.

The loving male side of both the Canticles spiritual tradition and the chivalry culture parallel the psychological need of the male to be dedicated to the female. This is needed in both the ideal and personal and is recognized in general by all social structures.[29] The southern cultural environment channeled the male-female need to the courtly love tradition in marriage.[30] The recognition of Father Price's dedication to celibacy and his coming from a society with a strong chivalry/love tradition provides an important backdrop to understanding his life's journey.

The South and Roman Catholicism

With fewer than two thousand Roman Catholics in North Carolina during the last half of the nineteenth century,[31] personal commitment to the Church had to be real and sincere in order to withstand the social pressure placed upon individuals by their Protestant neighbors. An article in *Truth* magazine identified the attitude as general hatred of "Romanism."[32]

An example of the negative reaction to the Church can be seen in what happened to Dr. Monks, a physician of Newton Grove, North Carolina, and his family when they converted to Roman Catholicism. The Protestant community was so angered that "at once the doctor and his wife were ostracized and excluded entirely from all social intercourse by his former friends, his lucrative practice fell away and he was reduced to some straights to support his then young and growing family."[33] The Church in the South was certainly a mission church.

Differences between Roman Catholics and Protestants came over an understanding of sacraments, church authority and devotion to the saints, especially the Blessed Virgin. With worship seen as superstitious, Roman policy counter to democratic principles, foreign priests as leaders, and civil unrest caused by Roman Catholic immigrants in the North, southerners feared that Romanism would upset their society.[34] Still Roman Catholics in the South were both pro-slave and supported the Confederacy.[35]

The southern religious environment with its hostility to Roman Catholics encouraged a devotion to church authority not only in doctrine and explanations of the faith but also in liturgical rubrics and spiritual practice.[36] In this environment conflicts can arise making conformity in minor matters very important. Father Price was strongly affected by the forces and mind-set created by this situation. As with many of his fellow believers, he was a true southerner or and a devout Roman Catholic.

Popular Spirituality

The mission church was also a church of the Counter-Reformation. It was highly centralized, parish oriented, and doctrinally focused.[37] While trying to demythologize the saints, it elevated the Blessed Mother and practices such as saying the Rosary and devotions to the Blessed Sacrament. Fred Price with his chivalry background was raised in a church where duty was important and where he saw no difference between the culture of the South and the church's demands. Doctrinally and ritually, it was a church under siege in the South.

Sacraments

In the Protestant South it was especially the sacrament of the Eucharist that was the focal point of misunderstanding and argument. Devotion to and acceptance of the Eucharist were encouraged among the Roman faithful. In the liturgy of Benediction, the practice of adoration of the Eucharist was important for it placed on the level of personal action and commitment what was being proclaimed on the level of doctrine.[38]

The Blessed Virgin

Certain events increased interest in the devotion to the Blessed Mother in the Roman Church at large. One of these key events was the appearance of the Blessed Mother to Bernadette Soubirous at Lourdes, France, in 1858.[39] The results of this increased devotional interest can be seen in the number of papal teachings issued on the Blessed Mother. Between 1740 and 1800 five teachings were issued. Between 1800 and 1850 there were six more, but between 1850 and 1900 twenty-seven teachings were issued. This trend continued to increase throughout the twentieth century.[40] A further example of the importance of this devotion of the Roman Catholic Church in the United States to the Blessed Mother is echoed in an 1887 book entitled *Catholic Gems* or "Treasures of the Catholic Church, a Repository of Catholic Instruction and Devotion" where 440 of its 1,066 pages are devoted to Mary.[41]

Cultural Change and Concreteness

But was the culture we have been describing the Old South, pre-1865, or the New South? Hasn't the South changed? As late as 1941, W. J. Cash wrote:

> The extent of change and break between the Old South [1607–1865] that was and the South of our time have been vastly exaggerated. The South, one might say, is a tree with many age rings, with limbs and trunk bent and twisted by all the winds of the years, but with its tap root in the Old South.[42]

How much closer was Fred Price, having been born in 1860, to that root?

The end of the Civil War, or the War of Northern Aggression as it is also known, did not diminish the role of chivalry and honor; rather it made it sacred. Southern culture was a way to preserve independence while joining the North in a political union.

Of course, to some the war has not ended. For example, in 1900 a young grandson of a Civil War veteran asked his grandfather: "Grandpa, the South won all the battles, but how did the war come out?"

"Sonny," said the old man, "it's too soon yet to tell."[43]

Throughout this study we must remember that southerners, and Fred Price in particular, are not role playing. What we have been talking about is not a masquerade. What is said and believed is to be acted upon. The term "concreteness" describes this mode of living and is part of the internal cultural debate.[44] Concreteness is so important that it can result in a fear of the abstract.[45]

The seriousness of chivalry and honor and the concreteness can be seen in the following. A mother asked about her sons going off to war knew the importance of honor. When asked: "Would you be happy if all the men in your family were killed?" She said: "Yes. If their life disgraced them. There are worse things than death."[46]

Notes

1. Thomas Frederick Price, ed., *Truth* 8:7 (July 1909) 181 and 8:8 (August 1908) 208.

2. William K. Tabb, ed., *Churches in Struggle* (New York: Monthly Review Press, 1986) xviii–xix; Anthony Kosnik, ed., *Human Sexuality* (Garden City, N.Y.: Doubleday, 1979) 11.

3. W. J. Cash, *The Mind of the South* (New York: Random House, 1969) 67–8.

4. John McBride Dabbs, *Haunted by God* (Richmond: Knox, 1972) 12–5, 19.

5. W. J. Cash, *The Mind of the South,* 67–8.

6. Robert E. Sheridan, ed., "The Very Reverend Thomas Frederick Price, Co-founder of Maryknoll, A Symposium 1956 with Supplement 1981" (Private printing, Brookline, Mass.: Brothers Novitiate, 1956, 1891) 99–100. It will be referred as *A Symposium.*

7. John Dabbs, *Haunted by God*, 33–6.

8. Bertram Wyatt-Brown, *Honor and Violence in the Old South* (New York: Oxford, 1986) 4.

9. Bertram Wyatt-Brown, *Honor,* 14.

10. Bertram Wyatt-Brown, *Honor,* viii.

11. Bertram Wyatt-Brown, *Honor,* 4.

12. Bertram Wyatt-Brown, *Honor,* 26.

13. Bertram Wyatt-Brown, *Honor,* 30.

14. Bertram Wyatt-Brown, *Honor,* 37.

15. John Dabbs, *Haunted by God,* 28.

16. Bertram Wyatt-Brown, *Honor,* 27.

17. W. J. Cash, *The Mind of the South,* 87–8.

18. Ibid., 89.

19. Bertram Wyatt-Brown, *Honor,* 28.

20. Bertram Wyatt-Brown, *Honor,* 35.

21. John Dabbs, *Haunted by God,* 34.

22. Jean LeClercq, *Monks on Marriage, A Twelfth Century View* (New York: Seabury, 1982) 2-3.

23. James B. Nelson, *Embodiment* (Minneapolis: Augsburg, 1978) 107.

24. Jean LeClercq, *Monks on Marriage,* 5.

25. Jean LeClercq, *Monks on Marriage,* 3–4, 79.

26. Andreas Capellanus, *The Art of Courtly Love,* trans. with introduction and notes by John Jay Parry (New York: Norton, 1941).

27. Maurice Valency, *In Praise of Love* (New York: Macmillan, 1958).

28. James B. Nelson, *Embodiment,* 107–8.

29. Sigmund Freud, *Civilization and Its Discontents* (New York: Norton, 1961) 55; Genesis 1:27-31; Genesis 2:22-25.

30. W. J. Cash, *The Mind of the South,* 76–7.

31. Unlike other southern states by 1860 North Carolina had so few Roman Catholics that it did not justify the establishment of a diocese. Randall M. Miller and Jon L. Wakelyn, *Catholics in the Old South* (Macon: Mercer, 1983) 68.

32. William B. Hannon, "Scattered Catholics in the South—Their Location and Their Duty," *Truth* 14:3 (March 1910) 73.

33. Robert Sheridan, ed., *A Symposium,* 113–4.

34. Miller and Wakelyn, *Catholics,* 17.

35. Miller and Wakelyn, *Catholics,* 16, 242–6.

36. Miller and Wakelyn, *Catholics,* 54.

37. Keith P. Luria, "The Counter-Reformation and Popular Spirituality," *Christian Spirituality: Post-Reformation and Modern,* Louis Duprè and Don F. Saliers, eds., (World Spirituality: An Encyclopedic History of the Religious Quest, vol. 18) New York: Crossroad, 1989, 93–120.

38. T. F. Price, ed., *Truth* 14:4 (April 1910) 124.

39. Thomas Frederick Price, ed., *The Lily of Mary: Bernadette of Lourdes* (New York: Bureau of the Immaculate Conception, 1918) 31.

40. The Benedictine Monks of Solesmes, *Our Lady* (Boston: Daughters of St. Paul, 1961) 580–91.

41. Francis DeLigny, Abbè Orsini, and John G. Shea, *Catholic Gems* (New York: Office of Catholic Publications, 1887).

42. W.J. Cash, *The Mind of the South*, x.

43. James Dabbs, *Haunted by God*, 18.

44. Robert B. Heilman, "The Southern Temper," *Southern Renascence,* Louis D. Rubin, Jr., Robert D. Jacobs, eds. (Baltimore: John Hopkins, 1953) 3–7.

45. C. Vann Woodward, "The Search for Southern Identity," *The South and the Sectional Image*, Dewey W. Grantham, Jr., ed. (New York: Harper & Row, 1967) 185–6.

46. Bertram Wyatt-Brown, *Honor*, 28.

3

The Groom: Childhood (1860–1877)

The South during the Civil War and the reconstruction era forms the backdrop for the early years of Thomas Frederick Price's life. His mother and father were from old southern families—English stock that was dedicated to the South. The war was harsh on Wilmington, North Carolina, where the Price family lived. There were problems of disease and shellings by Union ships; at one point the Price family had to leave the city. With the loss of the war, damage to the city, the arrival of carpetbaggers, and Union military occupation, the Price children's first introduction to northerners was not positive. In addition, the awareness and discussion of these events and situations in the Price household would have been greater than in most southern families because Mr. Price was a newspaper editor.

The Price Family

Freddie, as Father Price was called by his family and close friends, was the eighth of ten children born to Alfred Lanier Price and Clarissa Bond.[1] Both parents were converts to Roman Catholicism. Clarissa Bond, who was born in Bath, North Carolina, in 1825, had to leave home when she converted from Methodism to Catholicism at age eighteen. In addition to being disinherited, she was prevented by her father from entering the convent of the Sisters of Charity at Charleston, South Carolina. Clarissa went to Washington, North Carolina, to live with Dr. and Mrs. Thomas Frederick Gallagher, who were Roman Catholics from Philadelphia.[2] Clarissa later married Alfred Lanier Price. They moved to Wilmington, where in 1851 he began publishing the *Wilmington Daily Journal*. Alfred, born an Episcopalian, became a Catholic on Christmas Day 1866.[3] In 1872 when Freddie Price was just twelve years old his father died. Alfred Price, as a newspaper publisher, had "been a leading citizen of Wilmington of his time," and it was said of him that "his labors have done as much to build up our thriving city as those of any of her citizens."[4]

Since Alfred Price was such a prominent citizen, there is little doubt that the Price children were raised as proper southerners. The boys would have been brought up as southern gentlemen in a culture that placed a high value on what it considered to be, proper male-female relationships. Fred was so much a part of the culture that a life-long friend wrote that he "was North Carolina incarnate."[5] This colorful and dynamic era of the South was the backdrop for the Price family.

The Church

It appears that the Church, particularly the parish of St. Thomas Cathedral in Wilmington, was a focal point of Freddie Price's youth. It provided his formal education, the foundational elements of much of his spirituality, and important personal contacts. Specifically, devotion to the Blessed Sacrament and the Blessed Mother and the personal relationship with James Cardinal Gibbons, all were to have a lifelong effect on his spiritual formation and theological development.

In 1867 the life-long relationship with James Gibbons began when the young bishop was assigned as the vicar of North Carolina. Fred was one of the regular altar boys for the bishop at Wilmington. It continued when Gibbons was archbishop of Baltimore and Freddie Price was a student at St. Charles' College and St. Mary's Seminary in Baltimore. Throughout his priesthood Fred made many visits to the cardinal's residence in Baltimore. This relationship was instrumental in gaining the American bishops' support for the founding of an American foreign mission seminary, later known as Maryknoll.

The involvement in the Church came from that most important of southern institutions the family and the "kinkeeper,"

Clarissa Bond Price, who was the spiritual leader of her family. She was dedicated in service to the local parish and to the religious vocations of her children.

Vocations

Two of Freddie's older sisters entered the religious life. Both Mary Elizabeth and Margaret became Sisters of Our Lady of Mercy in Charleston, South Carolina.[6] This was the same religious order that Clarissa Price had wanted to join as a young girl.

Prior to entering the convent, the two older sisters, Mary and Margaret, taught in the Catholic school that was in the basement of the cathedral at Wilmington. Freddie attended that school rather than the public school.[7] Later Mary Elizabeth Price, as Sr. Mary Catherine, led the first group of sisters in the running of the orphanage that was founded by her brother Freddie at Nazareth, North Carolina in 1900. It appears that his older brother Willie (William Pascal Price, 1853–1904) attended St. Charles College, a junior seminary in Baltimore from 1871–1875.[8]

While Freddie was very young there is a story concerning his call to the priesthood. The following is the often noted[9] conversation between Freddie and his pastor, Fr. Mark Gross:

> Father Gross one day asked him [Freddie Price]: "Would you like to be a priest?" The zealous shepherd of souls was not a little surprised at the answer: "I would. And I want to be a very good priest, too!"
>
> "Then," said the other, when he caught his breath, "you ought to begin saying five Our Fathers and five Hail Marys every day, for the intention of becoming a very good priest."
>
> If he had been surprised at Freddie's first response, Father Mark was destined for yet another when the boy answered very innocently.
>
> "But, Father, I have already been doing that for a long time."[10]

The Blessed Mother

Marian devotion was an important part of Fred's early understanding of prayer and the foundation stone of his spiritual development.

Clarissa Bond Price was the first person to introduce the Price family, particularly the children, to Marian spirituality and Marian devotions.[11] For the young Clarissa Bond the Catholic teaching on the Blessed Mother had been a block to her conversion, but once she accepted it she developed a love for the Blessed Mother and passed it on to her children.[12]

If there was one thing that all those who knew Fred Price agreed upon, it was that he was devoted to the Blessed Virgin.[13] Personal use of Marian devotions and prayers such as the Rosary and novenas were life-long practices for Fred. One of the images of Father Price in the memories of those who know him from his time at Nazareth (1900–1910) was his walking the grounds in the evening saying the Rosary.[14] Saying the Rosary was part of the daily prayer cycle established during the retreat of 1908. While at the conferences in Rome discussing the new American mission society (1911–1919), Father Price said the Rosary.[15] Reflections by associates at Maryknoll in Ossining and at Maryknoll's preparatory seminary, the Venard, in Scranton noted his use of the Rosary.[16] Novenas, including those to the Blessed Mother, are mentioned throughout his life. It is difficult to understand the relationship that later develops between the Blessed Mother and Fred without positing prior catechesis and devotional experience established during his childhood.

Healings and Visions

Clearly Clarissa Bond Price provided a spiritual background and interest in vocations that fueled the religious drive in the Price family. She was so influential that she "is mentioned in O'Connell's *Catholicity in the Carolinas and Georgia* as one of the prominent laywomen in Wilmington during the 1860s."[17]

She guided the children towards a religious or priestly vocation and provided a Catholic oriented education in an anti-Roman, southern environment. In addition, there are two noteworthy spiritual events that surround the end of Clarissa's life, which were near the end of Fred's studies in Baltimore in 1886.

First, there is the healing of an old pastor, Father Moore, who asked Clarissa, while on her deathbed, to speak to God when she met him and ask God to give him his sight back so that he could say Mass again. The day after her death, he was able to say Mass.[18]

Shortly after her death, during a Mass Clarissa's young grandson saw his grandmother with a man on one side and a beautiful lady on the other. After this event and through the work of Dr. Corcorcan, Pope Pius IX pronounced the Price family to be a "holy family."[19] Verification of the healing and vision is difficult at this distance from the event. However, they were taken very seriously and accepted by the local parish and Church authorities at the time.

Notes

1. Robert E. Sheridan, ed., *A Symposium*, S–11.

2. Patrick J. Byrne, *Father Price of Maryknoll* (Maryknoll, New York: Catholic Foreign Mission Society of America, 1923) 4–5.

3. Raymond A. Lane, *The Early Days of Maryknoll* (New York: David McKay Company, 1951) 57; John C. Murrett, *Tarheel Apostle* (New York: Longmans, 1944) 7–8.

4. Robert E. Sheridan, ed., *A Symposium*, S–6, S–7.

5. Robert E. Sheridan, ed., *A Symposium*, 99.

6. John C. Murrett, *Tarheel Apostle*, 42.

7. Patrick J. Byrne, *Father Price*, 9.

8. Robert E. Sheridan, ed., *A Symposium*, 20.

9. It is recorded as early as 1923 in Patrick J. Byrne's *Father Price of Maryknoll*, 8.

10. John C. Murrett, *Tarheel*, 8–9.

11. Patrick J. Byrne, *Father Price*, 4.

12. Patrick J. Byrne, *Father Price*, 4.

13. Many of the testimonies gathered for the symposium in 1956 mention this devotion to the Blessed Mother.

14. John C. Murrett, *Tarheel*, 58.

15. John C. Murrett, *Tarheel*, 109.

16. He would make a six-mile pilgrimage from Maryknoll to Hawthorne's Lourdes' Grotto saying the Rosary. John Murrett, *Tarheel*, 154, 161–2.

17. Robert E. Sheridan, ed., *A Symposium*, S–7.

18. Patrick J. Byrne, *Father Price*, 13.

19. Patrick J. Byrne, *Father Price,* 13–4. The incident as reported by John Murrett in *Tarheel Apostle* (19) is a little different. There is no mention of the other women in the vision. The older version as reported by Byrne has been selected.

4

The Groom: Sulpician Education
Baltimore (1877–1886)

The Sulpician education at St. Charles College and St. Mary's
Seminary had a major impact on Fred Price. His education both
opened and closed experiential and expressive theological paths
for him.

Between 1877 and 1886 Fred was exposed to a variety of
spiritual traditions in addition to the overall Sulpician approach
to religious education. They include the book *Following Christ*,
the Marian devotions of Louis de Montfort and, through
Cardinal Gibbons and the Baltimore Carmel, the spiritual tradition of St. Teresa of Avila and St. John of the Cross. This
Baltimore phase of Fred Price's life was bracketed by several
major spiritual events.

SS Rebecca Clyde Event

In September 1876 Fred Price set sail from Wilmington for
Baltimore in order to begin studies at St. Charles College.* As the
vessel was moving north along the North Carolina coast, it floun-
dered in a storm.

Mr. W. L. Parsley of Wilmington was a passenger aboard the
Clyde when it went down on September 16, 1876. On September

---

*Our objective here is not to establish the validity of the events sur-
rounding the sinking of the SS Rebecca Clyde. Rather it is to establish
clearly what seventeen-year-old Freddie Price would say was real.

26 he wrote to his niece, Miss Anna Savage, and recounted his "adventure" and mentioned that there were six passengers, one of them being Fred Price. The ship was caught in a severe storm near Ocracoke Inlet, south of Cape Hatteras, North Carolina. The crew and one passenger named Joe, a friend of Mr. Parsley, had depleted the supply of life preservers. The letter tells of the ship's breaking-up and his struggle to get ashore:

> As soon as I found myself all safe, I went up the beach in search of Joe, not knowing whether he was safe or not, but was unable to find him for some time and had started up to houses when I saw him coming to meet me. Joe had succeeded in getting a life-preserver and swam ashore all right, but without other support. But how little Fred Price got ashore was certainly miraculous. He could not swim a lick. He says when washed overboard he caught hold of a spar while under water and succeeded in holding on until washed ashore.
>
> It is strange that out of five from Wilmington (namely, two soldiers from Smithville, Fred Price, Joe and myself) we were all saved.[1]

Fred Price returned home to Wilmington. After recovering from the exhausting experience, he went to St. Charles College in February 1877. Fortunately while at St. Charles he confided in one of his classmates William H. O'Connell, later the cardinal-archbishop of Boston. He recalls a conversation with Fred Price:

> I shall never forget the story of an incident that happened to him [Freddie Price] on his voyage from somewhere in the South to Baltimore, on his way to enter St. Charles's. . . . Presently the customary smile appeared on his face, and after making me promise to tell no one, he gave me in confidence the full narration of what was undoubtedly a manifestation of God's love of him and a special protection of the Blessed Virgin.
>
> Bashfully, in a quiet but assured tone of voice, this young saint related the authentic story which thrilled me to the depths of my soul. I cannot here reproduce the simple yet tremendously moving picture then portrayed by him. . . .
>
> Keeping his head as best he could, with all his physical strength, above the furious waters, he cried again, "Christ Jesus, save me or I perish." Like a flash the sky seemed to open, and out

of a speck of blue came the clearest possible vision, as clear as he saw the howling waves about him—Mary, the Mother of Christ, appeared before his eyes. Upon her face was a smile, and gently stretching forth her hand, she pointed to a great floating plank, which had been washed overboard from the sinking ship. Strengthened superhumanly by the perfect confidence of safety, he gained the plank, pulled himself upon it, threw himself face forward upon it and grasping a great ring on its upper surface, he swung, now up, now down, in the great waves about him, feeling nothing and thinking now and then of the vision, which would always remain indelibly imprinted on his soul. He began the Litany of the Blessed Virgin, and he said, "In my joy I almost sang it."[2]

Cardinal O'Connell was correct about the event being imprinted upon Fred's soul. Father Price mentioned the incident on August 25, 1908 in the fourth letter in the *Diary* he wrote to the Blessed Mother:

I saw a piece in "[The] Field Afar" that made me happy. It was that Father Juste Bretennier [Juste de Bretenieres]—the French Martyr Priest—had a vision, natural or otherwise—of the Chinese beckoning him to Martyrdom when he was about 5 years. It brought vividly to my mind the imagination I had of you, Mother, when I was shipwrecked and under the water and I called your sweet and loved form to my mind, and it made me reflect that my whole life at this time and ever after has been dependent on you, and [I] recalled what you seemed to promise at my last retreat {August 1908}. My shipwreck and the worse time I had after—my present work—my society—my whole being and work, O my Mother, are truly yours, and this knowledge and dwelling on it this afternoon after reading Father Juste [de] B. made me very happy.[3]

It is an understatement to say that the vision of the Blessed Mother during the sinking of the Clyde had an effect on Father Price's life.

Reflections

In looking at the documentation concerning the Clyde incident, there are multiple sources of the event. There is no doubt that the event did happen and that Fred Price who could not swim did survive the disaster without a life preserver. As for the vision of the Blessed Mother, there is little reason to doubt the sincerity of our sources. William O'Connell would have gained little by fabricating such a story and putting it in his memoirs. Fred's own mention of the event in the *Diary* would not offer an occasion to misrepresent or fabricate the vision since there were personal and private letters to the Blessed Mother who in his mind and heart was at the event.

During the event itself there is a non-projection of the vision by Fred Price who claimed that he called for Jesus, only to have the Blessed Mother appear. That Mary showed up for Jesus is consistent with the expressive theology or doctrine Fred had and would be taught. Rather than praying to the Blessed Mother in order to communicate with Jesus, it was salvation requested of Jesus that came through the Blessed Mother.

To Fred Price, and others such as William O'Connell who personally accepted his story, we have an illumination not of God or the divine but rather of a saint. But does this experience mean that Fred experienced a "deep mystical conversion"?

Several factors go into making up a mystical or spiritual conversion experience (see appendix A). According to Evelyn Underhill there is a sense of liberation or victory, awareness of the nearness of God, an outpouring of love for God, and a non-egocentric world view.[4] On the surface the Clyde experience looks as if it were a true spiritual conversion experience with the liberation from the water and with Fred's belief that the Blessed Mother was truly there, so much so that he dedicated his life to her. There is still, however, a focus on what Thomas Frederick Price was doing for the Blessed Mother and not on what she or God wanted done. In this case the dedication is to a most important saint, rather than to God directly. Additionally the event, while yielding a dedication,* did not radically change the perception that Fred Price had of the world.[5] He was doing his duty via intellectual dedication, planning, working, and proclaiming. The duty was certainly part of the requirement of a

*The dedication is seen later in his life in the acceptance of Marian devotions and in the naming of churches and locations in North Carolina, New York, and China.

southern gentleman and was no more of an effort than that which he had already begun by heading towards St. Charles College.

Over the years Father Price's personal dedication to the Blessed Mother continued to grow, and in 1908 he addressed her as "My own loved Mother" in the *Diary* letters. It would be in 1911 at Lourdes that he would truly have a conversion experience and then have a very different view of the world and dedicate his total inner being to the Blessed Mother, Bernadette, and God. The spiritual event surrounding the sinking of the Clyde was quite a beginning to the educational process that was to lead him to priesthood.

Sulpician Influence

It was February 1877 before Fred Price finally arrived at Baltimore, where he spent the next nine years studying at the Sulpician founded and staffed schools of St. Charles College, the preparatory seminary, and St. Mary's Seminary. The French Sulpician Fathers had founded the schools as part of their missionary effort in the United States. The schools reflected their founder's unique philosophy of education. Fred Price spent four years at St. Charles, graduating in 1881. That same year he began studies at St. Mary's Seminary; he completed the major seminary course of studies in June 1886. For Fred Price to have completed the course of study at St. Charles and St. Mary's was a credit to both the support he received from home and his own personal dedication. Of Fred's contemporaries, only 36 percent made it through the entire process and were ordained.[6]

The curriculum at St. Charles was that of a fine, traditional, classical college of the era. However, religious instruction was not emphasized.[7] This type of education emphasized the Greek and Latin classics and philosophy. This was the proper college education for a southern gentleman, who as an educated man should be able to quote from the classics of western civilization. In addition to the classics, the Sulpicians required six years of French. There is no indication that Fred Price was an outstanding student or benefited from foreign language study.[8]

Theological Studies

Great scholar, linguist or not, the importance of the curriculum that Fred Price studied in Baltimore cannot be ignored. There was *not* extensive religious instruction at St. Charles College, the preparatory seminary, or at St. Mary's Seminary. Fred attended these Sulpician schools just before the blossoming of the theological faculty. It was not until a year or so after Fred Price graduated that the school reached the "manual of theology stage" of theological instruction with the arrival of Adolphe Tanquerey in 1887.[9]

At St. Mary's before 1886 (Father Price's graduation year) there "existed in the seminary only a single course of dogma and one of moral theology. This meant that all the students of dogma, whether of the first or third year, followed the same course of lectures, the same being true for the students of morals."[10] The texts used for instructing dogmatic and moral theology were the popular catechisms of the time. While Father Price was attending both schools, the Collot and DeHarbe catechisms were used.[11]

Theological Integration

While not central to the academic programs, theological and religious instruction were the emphasis of the chapel program. This approach to seminary training had a significant impact on Fred Price's spiritual and theological formation:

> The Sulpicians have always regarded the chapels of their seminaries as an important educational element. We are therefore prepared to see them devote much taste, attention and money to the chapel of St. Charles' College. . . . In 1855, when other provision had been made for the external congregation, a new chapel for the students was opened on the second floor, where divine worship was conducted with becoming dignity and impressiveness.[12]

The Sulpician chapel program used the method of St. Sulpice, which integrated the learning of doctrine and devotions. The singing of hymns and recitation of the Scriptures and prayers were a key part of the program.[13] This type of training, with its strong integration of doctrine and devotion, was a method toward sanctification.

Since doctrine was to be learned and proclaimed, the ongoing development of creative elements in exploring the theological meaning of the doctrinal statements emerges on the experiential side of theology. This truly reflects Father Price's life and his need to integrate expressional and experiential theology. The Sulpician method calls for the resolution of the conflicts within oneself. It therefore can cause a personal spiritual-theological crisis in that it demands that expressive and experiential theology be closely aligned. However it does prevent a long-term, intra-personal spiritual-theological split within the individual. This demand for unity and integration that parallels the southerner's need for concreteness and call to duty later ferments a crisis for Fred concerning his Marian devotional prayer and the requirement that prayer be trinitarian (i.e., was Marian prayer doctrinally acceptable).

This integrated approach to experiential and expressional theology would help keep Fred within the boundaries of acceptable Catholic mission proclamation and practice. The formal spiritual practices that Fred Price used while attending the Sulpician schools were the Mass, the Rosary, novenas, and benediction, which deepened the devotional and religious experience that he had from his youth in North Carolina. The Sulpicians gave Fred Price both the reverence for liturgy and the need for prayer that is attested to by many who knew him.[14]

Following Christ

When Fred Price was first introduced to Thomas à Kempis's *Imitation of Christ* (known to Father Price as *Following Christ*) cannot be determined. Since he quotes it often in the early issues of *Truth,* uses it for spiritual meditations with the students at Maryknoll, and refers to it in the *Diary,* it is probably safe to assume that his first reading of the book was while he was studying in Baltimore.[15] From the numerous quotations in *Truth,* Father Price emphasized the purgation needed in *Following Christ* and the need to pursue seeking the Lord. As the years of editing *Truth* went on, the use of *Following Christ* as a filler text declined. The book appears to have contributed to his under-standing of the purgative way and to a spiritual approach to the Eucharist. Long, sincere dedication to the host during the Mass was noted by those around him. On several occasions in the *Diary* he notes that this time was used to make special dedications.[16]

Marian Devotion

In addition to their attention to the Mass and adoration of the Blessed Sacrament, the Sulpicians held a particular love for and devotion to the Blessed Mother.[17] It is difficult to identify when Fred Price was introduced to the writing of de Montfort and the devotional exercises called *The Little Office of the Blessed Virgin Mary.* He might have even been introduced to them by Father Gross, his pastor in Wilmington who also graduated from St. Mary's.[18] At least he began to use the *Little Office* and Marian writings as regular sources of devotional practice while at St. Charles' and St. Mary's.

The Little Office

It is believed that the *Little Office* has been used in the Western Church for centuries. Possibly dating back to the 700s and has been in more or less the same form since the 1500s.[19] The prayers of the Office are based on seven sessions or hours paralleling the monastic hours. With some variation the basic "hour" follows this framework:

1. A silent Hail Mary
2. Sign of the Cross
3. Introductory prayer(s)
4. Psalm(s)
5. A short Scripture reading
6. A hymn and/or oration and a blessing
7. A closing prayer

Advent, Christmas, Lent and Easter variations are also given. Intended for the laity, or other non-monastics, the sessions could be combined if necessary. The prayers themselves, while having a

"God" focus, also have a Marian orientation. They include a daily proclamation that Mary is ever-virgin and emphasize the Blessed Mother's closeness to the Trinity. The prayer form is that of a condensed monastic breviary that has a Marian orientation. The following prayer is an example:

> O blessed Mother of God, Mary ever virgin, temple of the Lord, sanctuary of the Holy Ghost: thou alone, without example, wast well pleasing to our Lord Jesus Christ. Pray for the people, mediate for the clergy, intercede for the devoted female sex.[20]

An example from the Oration at Prime proclaims the Blessed Mother's closeness to the Trinity.

> Let us pray: O God, who didst vouchsafe to choose the chaste chamber of the Blessed Virgin Mary in which to dwell; grant, we beseech thee, that, fortified with the defense, we may find our joy in taking part in her commemoration. Who livest and reignest with the Holy Ghost, world without end.[21]

It is not clear when *The Little Office of the Blessed Virgin Mary* was introduced to Father Price or when he began to pray it daily. However, it appears to have predated his time at Nazareth for he was seen daily in the chapel saying it along with the Divine Office.[22] His devotion to the Blessed Mother and familiarity with both the works of William Faber which appeared in *Truth,* and Louis de Montfort, combined with the Sulpician dedication to the Blessed Mother and Fred Price's own focusing experience, indicates that he probably started praying the *Little Office* daily while in the seminary.

De Montfort

Again the exact date at which Fred Price was exposed to the writings of Louis de Montfort cannot be determined. However, with the deep devotion to the Blessed Virgin among the Order of St. Sulpice,[23] particularly at St. Charles and St. Mary's,[24] and Fred Price's personal commitment to the Blessed Mother from age seventeen, it would be safe to assume that he had read Louis de

Montfort's *True Devotion to the Blessed Virgin Mary* while at
school in Baltimore.

The practice of consecration of oneself to Mary is encouraged by de Montfort.[25] Saying prayers to the Blessed Mother, including daily recitation of the Rosary was also encouraged.[26]
While external activity was to be avoided since true devotion was
in the heart, the wearing of "little chains" was laudatory: "It is a
most glorious and praiseworthy thing, and very useful to those
who have thus made themselves slaves of Jesus in Mary, that they
should wear, a sign of their loving slavery, little iron chains,
blessed with the proper blessing."[27]

There are three reasons for wearing chains as a reminder of
one's baptismal vows: to show that one is not ashamed of slavery
to Jesus Christ,* to renounce sin, and to protect one against the
chains of sin and the devil.[28] Being a slave of Jesus in Mary focuses on the incarnation and the intimate union between them.[29]
Jesus's being in Mary is seen as the total union of the two.
Acceptance of this union is full acknowledgement of the incarnation. Therefore the more one allows "Mary to act in your
Communion, the more Jesus will be glorified."[30] However it was
not de Montfort's writings that enkindled the personal devotion
to the Blessed Mother by Fred Price; rather it was the dynamic
event in the sea off the North Carolina coast that happened prior
to his arrival at St. Charles that was to give him a life of personal
devotion to Mary.

The Carmelites

While Cardinal Gibbons was archbishop of Baltimore, he would
visit the Baltimore Carmel, and it was his practice to take seminarians along to assist him as altar boys. Fred Price was a logical
choice for such a duty having had prior experience. This
Carmelite exposure would explain the extensive use of the writings of Teresa of Avila and John of the Cross in *Truth* magazine

---

*Slavery as used by Fred Price appears to mean a total commitment
in spirit and fact to Jesus' and Mary's will. This is a personal voluntary
commitment out of a desire to fully dedicate oneself, not an imposed
slavery as practiced in secular society.

years later and the fact that in 1911 Father Price went to the Carmel to pray during the bishops discussion on proposing to Rome that an American foreign mission seminary be established. Furthermore, it explains the personal ongoing relationship that he had with some of the sisters of the Baltimore Carmel, a relationship that continued through 1918 and Fred's departure for China.

Teresa's and John's writings have a strong call to purgation and poverty in seeking the Lord. Through the Carmelite writings Fred Price was introduced to the concept of spiritual marriage and union with Christ. St. Teresa paints the image of one being in total union with Jesus and calls for being a saint. These concepts would offer a setting to Father Price and make Bernadette's request to be wed fit within the expressive theology to which he had some exposure.

Cardinal Gibbons

In addition to accompanying Cardinal Gibbons to the Baltimore Carmel, Fred had an opportunity to work with the bishops of United States during his last year at St. Mary's. The occasion was the Third Plenary Council of the Roman Catholic Bishops of the United States hosted by the cardinal at the seminary.[31] This experience increased Fred's knowledge of the American rubrics and the bishops' understanding of current issues.

Healings

As a deacon at St. Mary's, Fred Price was faced with a crisis. As a result of a severe cold, he was going deaf and feared that he would be disqualified for ordination to the priesthood (Fred's concern was not without foundation for his spiritual director confirmed that if he was deaf his life-long desire to be a priest might not be fulfilled). Again he reached out for help to his supernatural mother. He began the novena of *Maria, Spes Nostra* (Mary, Our Hope). By the end of the ninth day of prayer, his hearing returned.[32] Again, at issue is not the actual event but the fact that Fred Price believed he was healed by the Blessed Mother.

The Sulpician educational years had a major impact upon Fred's spiritual formation. Bracketed by the Marian events of the Clyde sinking and a healing novena, the chapel/catechism method of education had reinforced his earlier spirituality and given him other prayer forms and texts to support it.

He was not a creative, scholarly theological thinker (not that the catechism level approach to theological studies encouraged such reflection) but educational experience reenforced his dedication to serving the Blessed Mother and the Church. In Baltimore he was exposed to the importance of liturgy, to Carmelite spirituality, and to a Marian spirituality. He not only owed his life but also his ministry to the Blessed Mother.[33] His ministry in North Carolina began on June 29, 1886 when at the pro-cathedral in Wilmington he was ordained a priest by Bishop H.P. Northrop.

Notes

1. George C. Powers (Biography of Fr. Thomas Frederick Price, untitled, unpublished manuscript, Maryknoll Society Archives, 1943) 12–5.

2. William H. O'Connell, *Recollections of Seventy Years* (Boston: Houghton, Mifflin, 1934) 62.

3. Thomas Frederick Price, *Father Price's Diary*, Robert E. Sheridan, ed., (Maryknoll, New York: Maryknoll Fathers, 1980) 8.

4. Evelyn Underhill, *Mysticism* (New York: Dutton, 1961) 176–9.

5. Evelyn Underhill, *Mysticism*, 178.

6. Charles G. Herbermann, *The Sulpicians in the United States*, (New York: Encyclopedia Press, 1916) 262.

7. Charles G. Herbermann, *The Sulpicians*, 258–9.

8. Despite extensive language study Fred lacked linguistic fluency. For example, when he was asking for assistance in rebuilding the Regina Apostolorum, the priests' mission center, after the fire at Nazareth in 1905, he did not write in French to the Paris Foreign Mission Society. He never mastered Chinese. (See the Rev. Thomas F. Price, Nazareth, N.C., to the Rev. J. Freri, D.C.L., New York City, December 7, 1908, Propagation of the Faith Papers, University of Notre Dame Archives, South Bend, Ind., and John C. Murrett, *Tarheel Apostle*, 224–6; George Powers, 216).

9. Charles G. Herbermann, *The Sulpicians*, 259, 319–20.

10. Charles G. Herbermann, *The Sulpicians*, 319.

11. Charles G. Herbermann, *The Sulpicians*, 259.

12. Charles G. Herbermann, *The Sulpicians*, 256.

13. *The Method of St. Sulpice* (London: Griffith Farran Browne, 1896) 18–29, 43, 340.

14. There are numerous references in the biographies and testimonies in *The Symposium.*

15. *Diary*, 1964.

16. *Diary*, 1043, 1308, 3168, 3325.

17. Charles G. Herbermann, *The Sulpicians*, 299.

18. Charles G. Herbermann, *The Sulpicians*, 308.

19. Charles G. Herbermann, et al., ed., *Catholic Encyclopedia*, (New York: Encyclopedia Press, 1910) s.v. "Little Office of Our Lady" by Lesie A. St. L. Toke.

20. *The Little Office of the Blessed Virgin Mary* (Chicago: Franciscan Herald Press, 1979) 28.

21. *The Little Office*, 37.

22. John C. Murrett, *Tarheel*, 57.

23. Louis Marie Grignon de Montfort, *True Devotion to the Blessed Virgin Mary*, (Bay Shore, New York: Montfort Fathers, 1949) 180.

24. Charles G. Herbermann, *The Sulpicians in the United States*, (New York: Encyclopedia Press, 1916) 299.

25. Louis de Montfort, *True Devotions*, 171–4.

26. Louis de Montfort, *True Devotions*, 183–5.

27. Louis de Montfort, *True Devotions*, 175.

28. Louis de Montfort, *True Devotions*, 177–8.

29. Louis de Montfort, *True Devotions*, 182.

30. Louis de Montfort, *True Devotions*, 200.

31. Charles G. Herbermann, *The Sulpicians*, 319.

32. Patrick J. Byrne, *Father Price*, 11–2; George C. Powers, *Biography*, 33–4.

33. John C. Murrett, *Tarheel*, 18–20.

5

Tarheel Ministry
(1886–1908)

Fr. Thomas Frederick Price was the first native North Carolinian
to be ordained to the diocesan clergy of that state.[1] His years of
ministry in the Tarheel State have three stages. The first is Fred's
parish and circuit work that started immediately after ordination
and continued until 1897 when he began full-time missionary activity. Then, came his founding of *Truth* magazine and the
Apostolic Company of North Carolina with its mission center
and orphanage at Nazareth on a hill just outside of Raleigh.
Finally, while still directing the activities at Nazareth, during a retreat at Belmont Abbey in western North Carolina in 1908, he
began to write daily letters to the Blessed Mother.

Parish Ministry (1886–1897)

After ordination Fred was assigned to various parishes in the
Tarheel state. With only several hundred Roman Catholics
statewide, these parishes often covered large areas and included
several missions. Even by 1905 Fred reports that there were only
4,500 Catholics, and the Church was struggling to survive.[2]

Fred's desire to proclaim the teachings of the Church meant
problems and tensions with the Protestant leaders such as the
ones that he encountered during his brief assignment in
Asheville. The details of the situation are not known, and he was
there for only a few months in 1886–1887.[3] However, the hostility of that part of the state to Catholic missionary work is seen in

the attacks on *Truth* from the Asheville area during its first few months of publication.[4]

There is little direct documentation concerning Fred's spiritual growth covering the years 1886–1897. It is obvious though that Fred's dedication to the Blessed Mother that began in childhood and grew at the seminary continued as he named the churches being erected under his pastorate after the Blessed Virgin. The church at Halifax was named the Church of the Immaculate Conception, and another in Goldsboro, St. Mary's Church. This practice continued with the site of the North Carolina Mission Center and Orphanage near Raleigh being called Nazareth. The Mission Training Center and priest's house at Nazareth was called the Regina Apostolorum ("Queen of the Apostles"). This Marian naming that continued throughout his life ended with Maryknoll's first mission post in China, "Lourdes."[5]

Mission Activity (1897–1910)

The missionary dedication to his fellow Tarheels was additionally fueled during an alumni retreat at St. Mary's in Baltimore when he met Fr. Walter Elliott, C.S.P.[6] Walter encouraged Price to establish a mission band to actively work on converting the Tarheel state. Shortly after this Father Price asked Bishop Haid, the vicar of North Carolina and abbot of St. Mary's Benedictine Monastery at Belmont, North Carolina, to release him from parish work to pursue an active missionary effort in the Tarheel state. With the bishop's reluctant blessing, Fred started another phase of his life.

With the number of Catholics in North Carolina in 1896 at approximately eight hundred,[7] Fred Price began full-time mission work in a personal way with total dedication. After receiving approval from the bishop, he climbed Mount Mitchell, the highest point in the state, and stayed overnight in prayer to dedicate himself to this missionary effort to make every Tarheel a Roman Catholic.[8] This is a significant example of his integrating ministry and spirituality. It parallels the call in *Truth* magazine to both a correct understanding of Catholicism and the proclamation of a proper spiritual life. This stands as tangible evidence of his need as a southerner and desire from his Sulpician education to integrate his expressional and experiential theologies. *Truth* and the new mission society were to be the main efforts of the Tarheel apostle through the year 1911.

TRUTH

The negative attitude towards Catholics and other non-Protestant groups was so deep in the culture that the North Carolina constitution of 1797 had a pro-Protestant article in it.[9] A Catholic priest was a novelty in the Old North State, and accounts indicate that Fred was a decent preacher. When he gave a mission, the Protestant audiences came back for several nights to listen to "Priest Price."[10] During these missions and in his traveling and knocking on doors, in fact, during his entire life in North Carolina, Fred came face to face with the hostility that his fellow Tarheels had for the Church.

Fred believed that much of the Protestant hostility was based on misunderstanding about the doctrine and devotional practices of the Church. To get the word out to the non-Catholic, Fred founded *Truth* magazine. The first issue was published in April 1897 at Sacred Heart Parish in Raleigh. This was a unique publication in that it was to be for an audience that did not necessarily want to read it, a hostile non-Catholic readership.

While reports of the magazine's popularity vary, it was positively received by Catholics and had a strong reaction from Protestants. Numerous letters concerning the Protestant reaction to *Truth* appeared in the secular press and were answered by Fred in *Truth*. Certainly the magazine would have been helpful to the Tarheel Catholics in explaining their Church to their non-Roman neighbors.

Glimpses of editor Price's expressional theology come through in the selection of items for the magazine and in the "Question Box" and the "fill-in" quotes at the end of long articles. Many of the quotes in the early issues are from Carmelite writings (Teresa of Avila and John of the Cross) and Thomas à Kempis's *Following Christ.*

MISSION SOCIETY—NAZARETH

Fred purchased an old plantation on a hill outside of Raleigh and named it "Nazareth." He had plans for a mission headquarters that included not only a missionary residence and training center for priests but also an orphanage and hospital (the hospital was never built). Using the old mansion, the orphanage was started first in 1900 with his sister, Mary Elizabeth (now Sr. Mary Catherine), as the first administrator. With the sisters running the orphanage, Father Price set about building a church and a priest mission center, Regina Apostolorum.

The mission training center and seminary opened with twenty-five students in 1901. Regina Apostolorum also housed the priests that were assigned to Nazareth. Its number increased in the summer to include a training program that provided a first-hand experience of southern mission ministry to seminarians from the North. It was not a plush school or mission headquarters for it embodied the poor and stark life of a missionary in love with poverty. This air of poverty was a direct reflection of Fred's spirituality and understanding of mission.[11]

During this time missions were given in many towns. Small chapels were established throughout the mission territory. These were, in reality, nothing more than "shacks" that would provide a shelter for priests as they moved around the state, a place to celebrate Mass, and an area to hold catechetical classes.

Fred Price stated the purpose of his mission band called the Apostolic Company of North Carolina to the Paris Foreign Mission Society when he was asking for funds to rebuild Regina Apostolorum in 1905:

> We are a band of priests, at present four in number, working under Rt. Rev. Bishop Haid, the Vicar Apostolic of North Carolina and are known as the Apostolate of Secular Priests of North Carolina. Our work is mostly on non-Catholics, though we have one or two poor small Catholic congregations under our charge. We have a center at Nazareth, N.C., from which we are endeavoring to radiate and to build up a dozen small missions. We also have in charge a Boys Orphanage and Industrial School here which with the aid of the Sisters of Mercy who are associated in our work we have built up, and the orphanage and School is in a flourishing condition.
>
> We also conduct two magazines, one for the orphanage, and another for the extension of Catholic faith, called *Truth*. This latter magazine, called *Truth*, has done a great deal of good, being an

instructive magazine explanatory of Catholic faith and reaching upwards of seventy-five thousand readers every month, forty thousand of whom, it is estimated are Protestant. Moreover we are striving to educate and train up a number of young men in our work for the purpose of extending it as far as circumstances permit. All this work has been founded and kept up at the cost of very great sacrifice and labor.[12]

Despite the number of students in 1901, it appears that Price was quite alone in this mission vision. The stories of both the dedication of the church and priests' center at Nazareth in 1902 and the role of the bishop after a fire of 1905 demonstrate this. When Bishop Haid came to bless the buildings at Nazareth, he blessed the Church of the Holy Name and not Regina Apostolorum. The bishop was "too tired" to bless Father Price's mission project (for a discussion of the relationship see appendix D, The Tarheel and the Abbot); Father Price did that himself the following day.[13] Haid was only nominally supportive of rebuilding the structure when it burned down in 1905. While his letter, printed in *Truth*, suggested that perhaps this work, in its way, would contribute to the Church's growth and encourage others to support the rebuilding, it made it imminently clear that parish priests were doing the most important work.[14] Haid endorsed without comment, Price's request to the Paris Foreign Mission Society for assistance in rebuilding the Regina Apostolorum building.[15] Despite this less-than-enthusiastic support, Fred Price remained a man of vision, remarking to one of the priests at Nazareth: "Our band of mission workers shall be spread over the United States and even beyond—into China. Who knows—we may even have a chance to become martyrs!"[16]

While Fred was director of the center at Nazareth, he attended two missionary conferences. At the first in Winchester, Tennessee, in 1901, he presented a paper entitled "Localized Work in Country Districts."[17] During the second conference in Washington D.C., in 1904, Fred Price's paper was entitled "Localized Mission Work—A View from the Field," a paper which showed his dedication to mission activity and to the Tarheel state.[18] It is at this conference that Father Price met the director of the Propagation of the Faith from the Boston

Archdiocese, Fr. James Anthony Walsh.* This meeting, along with prayerful reflection, led Father Price to continue expanding his mission vision of first North Carolina, then the United States, China, and martyrdom.[19]

Notes

1. Patrick J. Byrne, *Father Price,* 14.

2. T. F. Price to J. Freri, December 7, 1908, Propagation of the Faith Papers, University of Notre Dame Archives.

3. Raymond A. Lane, *The Early Days of Maryknoll* (New York: David McKay Company, 1951) 58–9.

4. *Truth* 3:1 (April 1899) 16–9.

5. Patrick J. Byrne, *Father Price,* 83–4; John C. Murrett, *Tarheel,* 202, T. F. Price, *Diary,* 3298.

6. John C. Murrett, *Tarheel,* 33.

7. John C. Murrett, *Tarheel,* 38.

8. John C. Murrett, *Tarheel,* 32–5.

9. Thomas Frederick Price, ed., *Truth,* 1897 issues.

10. Patrick J. Byrne, *Father Price,* 24.

11. John C. Murrett, *Tarheel,* 58.

12. T. F. Price to J. Freri, December 7, 1908, Propagation of the Faith Papers, University of Notre Dame Archives.

13. George C. Powers, *Biography,* 88.

14. *Truth* 8:6 (May 1905) 234.

15. Bishop Leo Haid to Rev. J. Freri, undated endorsement to December 7, 1906 letter, Propagation of the Faith Papers, University of Notre Dame Archives.

16. John C. Murrett, *Tarheel,* 59.

17. The Catholic Mission Union, *Proceedings of the Winchester Convention* (New York: Office of the Missionary, 1901); John C. Murrett, *Tarheel,* 47–9.

18. *The Washington Conference* (Washington, D.C.: Washington Mission Union, 1906) 17, 31, 116–26.

19. John C. Murrett, *Tarheel,* 59.

*Walsh presented a paper on foreign missions. He was the editor of a magazine called *The Field Afar,* which was concerned with foreign missionary activity. He was to become co-founder of Maryknoll with Fred Price.

6

Tarheel Ministry
(1908–1911)

This second part of Fred Price's ministry in the Tarheel state begins with a spiritual event that set his course for the encounters at Lourdes in 1911. That event was the priest retreat of 1908. In September 1908 Fred attended a retreat for the priests of the Diocese of North Carolina at Belmont Abbey. This retreat was a major spiritual event for him in which for him Marian and Jesuit traditions came together. Some of the direct effects include the beginning of his daily personal discussion with the Blessed Mother, the establishment of a personal spiritual activity cycle, and dedication to the Ignatian Exercises. These elements are important in understanding Fred's future spiritual development.

The Letters

The singularly most important thing to emerge from the retreat was the commitment to the Blessed Mother of a daily letter. The letters summarize each day's activity and include spiritual experiences, health situations, pain, spiritual desires, fears, major events and problems, and future plans.* These letters have come to be called a *Diary,* but it is not a typical diary. The entries are, in fact, individual personal letters that focus on his spiritual concerns and

*See Appendix B for more information concerning the *Diary* and its use.

reveal the depths of his personal perceptions of self and others. In reading the 3,087 letters, one is immediately struck with the sincerity of this personal relationship that Fred clearly feels with the Blessed Mother. To call this collection a "diary" is misleading and does not do it justice.

There was a sincere desire by Fred Price to lead a life of prayer. The spiritual cycle he followed has a two-pole focus: one is Jesus Christ and the other is the Blessed Mother. Examples of this are found in the daily cycle of prayer that appears in the retreat notes on the first few pages of the *Diary:*

DAILY:

Office	Before the Blessed Sacrament
The Rosary	Before the Blessed Sacrament
Meditation	One hour (Ignatian Exercises)
Spiritual Reading	1/2 hour
2 Particular Examines	1/4 hour each
Study/Review of Moral Theology or Rubrics	1/4 hour (carefully done)

WEEKLY:

Confession	(well made)

RETREATS:

1 Day Retreat	Monthly
2 Day Retreat	Semi-annually
10–14 Day Retreat	Annually

ADDITIONAL:

As much time as possible in prayer
Join the Eucharistic League
If possible one hour before Eucharist for people before each sermon.[1]

This prayer cycle, with only minimal changes, Fred kept throughout his life. The modifications that he made were to increase daily time spent in prayer, spiritual reading, and reflection.

The routine structure of the letters give an insight into Fred's thought. The salutation to the Blessed Mother in these letters is

"My Own Dear Mother." The closings began with "Your sinful but loving son," and they ended with the signature "T.F.N." ("Thomas Frederick of Nazareth"). On August 29, 1908, he signed the letter: "T.F.N. of Jesus and Mary."[2] The next day he signed the letter "T.F.N. of Jesus." This was used for over three years through September 9, 1911.[3] As a southerner, Fred needed to belong to a "place." That place was now Nazareth. It gave him not only a sense of belonging but also an identity and the basis for honor that is so much a part of southern culture (see chapter 2).

In addition to a consistent salutation, closing, and signature, Fred Price often ended the letters with the same sentence. The development of this sentence can be seen in the letters of late August 1908:[4]

> Praise be to you and Jesus forever and ever! (August 22)
>
> Praise, honor and glory to you and Jesus, the only Love of my Heart, for ever and ever! (August 24)
>
> Love and praise to you and Love for ever and ever. (August 25)
>
> Praise be to you and Jesus my Love for ever and ever. (August 26)

These sentences were used throughout the letters with only minor changes from day to day. All proclaim praise to the Blessed Mother and Jesus "for ever and ever." The name "Jesus" is interchanged with "Love" at will. The earliest incident of Fred using "Love" that way is in a letter that was placed in the cornerstone in the original Regina Apostolorum.[5]

Price writes at the end of his retreat notes in the beginning of the *Diary*:

> My own dear Mother (The Blessed Virgin Mary) seemed to promise these things at the end of the retreat (1) That I should be fully hers and having only Jesus living in me henceforth and forever and that I should shed my blood—die a Martyr to Him whom my soul loves solely (2) That I should convert N.C. at least in lato sensu (3) that my society should be fully established (4)

that my present band (priests from outside permitted by Bp.)
should be properly founded (5) That Woods would go through
O.K. (6) That my ears would be cured and perhaps Woods* too.[6]

In the letters the loss of his own mother, who had been the
family kinkeeper and whose own death had been surrounded by
the special Marian events and who heightened his attachment to
the Blessed Mother, are noted. Certainly by 1908 the Blessed
Mother is totally accepted in the "mothering/kinkeeper" role by
Fred Price. More than just a personal dedication to the Blessed
Mother, Fred brought a focused commitment founded in the
spirituality he was exposed to during his years in Baltimore. The
commitment was one of total dedication to her, to Jesus, and to
the Church's teachings. He dedicated himself to her not only by
declaring her glory through naming the churches he built,[7] but
also through daily recitation of the Rosary and the Little Office
of the Blessed Virgin Mary throughout his life.[8] Fred's dedication
to the Blessed Mother in everything can be seen in the "Prospectus
to Truth" that appears in many of the issues: "Unto the honor of
the Blessed Virgin and under her patronage, we launch upon the
waters of religious journalism our little craft. . . ."

Jesuit Spirituality

During the retreat of 1908 Father Price made a sincere rededica-
tion to Ignatian spirituality. This interest was not new, nor did it
replace Marian spirituality; rather it became a layer on top of the
Marian devotions. Father Price used Ignatian spirituality as the
basis for the missionary spirituality at Nazareth. In a letter to Fr.
Michael Irwin, Fred expressed his intention to establish the apostolate based upon the Society of Jesus.[9] In fact, he had Fr. Edward
O'Rouke, S.J., give a thirty-day Ignatian retreat to the priests and
students at Regina Apostolorum in August 1905.[10] Later during
the discussions of the founding of a foreign mission seminary
with James Anthony Walsh in 1910, Price declared his desires to
use Ignatian spirituality as the spiritual basis for the new seminary. The seminary itself, however, was more important than the

---

*Fr. George Woods was the assistant at Nazareth.

specific use of Ignatian spirituality[11] and therefore it was not adopted as part of the rule for the new foreign mission society. Still for Fred the Ignatian Exercises were the foundation for the mission and his guide for purgations, striving to be a saint, and spiritual discernment. From August 1908 to August 1911, Fred desired to make a thirty-day retreat.[12]

While he was in Rome, he visited the tomb of St. Aloysius at St. Ignatius' Church.[13] After success in getting approval from the authorities in Rome to begin an American foreign mission society, Fred made arrangements for a thirty-day Ignatian retreat in Dublin, Ireland. En route to Dublin he stopped off at Lourdes, an action that radically changed his life and caused him to give up the Ignatian spirituality to which he had been so dedicated. Fred Price's dedication to the Ignatian exercises should not be surprising in light of the Sulpician method of teaching.[14]

However, prior to July 1911 there was a sincere commitment to the prayer cycle (quoted above) and the Ignatian Exercises.[15] The exercises however were the means to the end: to be a saint. The letters return to this specific objective several times.[16] In 1909 he describes being a saint as belonging to Jesus and the Blessed Mother, i.e., "to be entirely Jesus," "buried in Him and the Blessed Mother."[17] This "belonging to" matures and is expressed in both purgations and seeking union.

Purgations

A recurring theme for Fred is his seeking only poverty, suffering, and humility (via the Ignatian Exercises).[18] This had variations which included a concept of martyrdom based on humility, suffering, and spreading Jesus' glory.[19] One of the key phases of Christian spirituality is purgation (see appendix A). One of the purgations known to have been used by Fred since the mid-1890s was sleeping on the floor instead of a bed and using a stone for a pillow.[20]

While assigned to Sacred Heart Parish in Raleigh to begin his mission activity, the housekeeper noted a stone and a whip in his closet. The stone was used for a pillow and the whip for self-mortifications. There are indications that Fred had strictly prayed the daily office for priests and had practiced mortification since leaving the seminary.[21]

When asked about Father Price's sleeping practices, the Maryknoll sisters said that, "it was common knowledge that he [Father Price] slept on the floor. Sister Mercedes said the pastor at Our Lady of Lourdes in Brooklyn told her that Father Price, during the times he stayed there while on promotion work, would muss his bed to look as though it had been slept in, then sleep on the floor. He said he had seen Father Price sleeping on the floor."[22] This ascetic practice caused physical problems, and by 1917, while he was at St. Joseph's Infirmary in Hot Springs, Arkansas, for treatment of his rheumatism, the physician recommended that Fred stop sleeping on the floor. When he did this the pain in his legs began to go away.[23] This was only part of his purgations that included beating with a whip and the wearing of chains. His personal asceticism was at times severe, but later, as spiritual director, he would not allow seminarians to practice any purgation for more than a short time.

The presence of the stone and the whip in 1897, and the later dedication to the Ignatian Exercises, with documentation beginning in 1904, implies the introduction of the Exercises into Fred Price's life. In fact, a 1905 letter mentions his desire to be a member of the Society of Jesus and to work for the conversion of North Carolina.[24] This points to a willing acceptance of the Exercises and their purgative way of spiritual growth. This situation reflects that Fred's understanding of the individual as other than the divine. Evelyn Underhill expresses this understanding: "The Self . . . realizes by contrast its own finiteness and imperfection, the manifold illusions in which it is immersed, the immense distance which separates it from the One. Its attempts to eliminate by discipline and mortification all that stands in the way of its progress towards union with God constitutes *Purgation:* a state of pain and effort."[25] Certainly Fred was consciously pursuing purgations, though he was not being innovative. Both the hard bedding and self-flagellation purgations can directly be traced to the Ignatian Exercises where they are suggested as penances.[26]

In addition to the above practices, Father Price prayed the Rosary every evening and made the Stations of the Cross every morning.

Poverty and Pain

Fred Price had a sincere and gentle way, loved poverty, had an iron stomach to handle the simple food, displayed love of Blacks, and was a careless and poor dresser.[27] Price's sincere love of poverty became his trade-mark and was a major part of how he conducted mission. Poverty was a way of life at Nazareth. The Regina Apostolorum building, along with the food, was simple. Poverty was further reflected in Fred's missionary lifestyle. As he traveled throughout central North Carolina in his worn clothes, he begged for food and slept in the shacks called "country chapels."

In the winter of 1908, he was seriously troubled with malaria.[28] This weakening and years of missionary work in rural North Carolina, with its sleeping on the ground or on the floor of a shack, eventually took its toll. As the years progressed, Fred increasingly suffered from rheumatism. The pain had increased so much by 1917 that Father Price went for treatment to the St. Joseph Infirmary in Hot Springs, Arkansas. While there he feared that he would not be able to carry on his work and prayed to the Blessed Mother to heal his illness. He seemed to improve somewhat, for in the *Diary* he wrote: "Today there was a great diminution of the rheumatic pain and it certainly looks as if you have answered our novena in a literal and remarkable way. . . ."[29]

After several months of treatment, he had recovered enough to resume work, but unfortunately the pain was still with him.[30] Later, in southern China, Fred Price was exposed to the very humid climate of the Yeungkong Valley. It made his rheumatism so bad that serious consideration was given to sending him back to the United States or at least Japan for treatment in hot baths.[31]

The air of poverty was heightened for Fred by the constant problem of getting money to cover operational costs at Nazareth. It was only operational money that was a problem. Money for land to build chapels and churches and expand the complex at Nazareth appeared to be readily available. He worried about money at Nazareth while he was journeying to Rome with James Anthony Walsh to discuss the founding of the foreign mission society with Vatican officials in 1911. Later he was concerned about money for his work spreading the news of Lourdes and the title of the Immaculate Conception for the Blessed Mother.

By October 1910 he linked suffering to martyrdom. He wrote in his letter to the Blessed Mother: "Praise to you, Mother, and our Love for whom I wish to lead a continuous martyred life—dying and suffering for souls to be brought to his glory—dying and suffering every day and every hour in the day."[32] A few days later Fred speaks of foreign missions and asks that his "blood be shed for our Love."[33] The continuous martyred life was seen in humiliations and purgations. Upon returning from a trip to Asheville, where he experienced animosity, Fred wrote: "I had the happiness of suffering many tortures of our Lord."[34]

Loneliness and Honor

The letters to the Blessed Mother between 1908 and June 1911 are filled with Fred's activity and his problem of loneliness. The loneliness stemmed from traveling alone on mission, being in charge of operations at Nazareth, having an innovative missionary vision and the general negative multi-level tension between himself and Abbot-Bishop Leo Haid. As a southerner the success or failure of a place reflected on the owner or leader. This affected Fred's personal honor. These activities also allowed him only a few close friends. One was Fr. Michael Irwin, a fellow priest of the vicariate who also used purgative practices.[35] Another was Paulist missionary Fr. Walter Elliot, who was a Yankee Civil War veteran.[36]

Traveling

Fred traveled long distances throughout central and eastern North Carolina. Some folks thought that he could bi-locate. He also made an increasing number of trips north to beg for funds. Through all this activity his inner desire to become a saint was becoming more and more intense.[37] Later he spent years traveling to promote Maryknoll. He always resented travel because it drained him spiritually and physically, yielding the feeling of non-accomplishment.

Leadership

At Nazareth, in addition to Fred's physical pain, there was the deep pain caused by another priest who was traitorous. This incident caused him to be determined to trust only Jesus and the

Blessed Mother.[38] There were those who spoke ill of him to the bishop and those who wanted to establish their own mission band after they had been trained in missionary concepts at Nazareth. Also some did not agree with the simple life of poverty that Father Price espoused.[39] He saw the problems at Nazareth both as humiliations and as blessings.[40]

Adding to the loneliness was that Fred was a visionary who desired to convert all of North Carolina's Protestants to Roman Catholicism. He had more than just a goal; he had a plan and a methodology.

Seeking Union

In addition to the feelings of honor, loneliness, and isolation, there was the loneliness of the spiritual quest during the North Carolina ministry years. Fred was not happy with his life of pride, ambition, envy, lust, meanness, lack of charity, and want of love and prayer.[41] The Ignatian Exercises helped guide him to resume using a stone pillow in May 1910. This produced in him a feeling of giving himself to Jesus.[42] He continually tried to increase his dedication to seeking only poverty, suffering, and humility.[43] This had variations which included a concept of martyrdom based on humility, suffering, and spreading Jesus' glory.[44]

As he strived to act and understand this commitment to belong to Jesus, Fred revealed his concept of discipleship as he sought men to work with him on his second missionary society venture. He wanted only those men who wanted to be a "copy of Jesus" and desired to be saints and apostles.[45]

The personal desire for saintliness continues throughout the *Diary*. In his midnight New Year's Eve letter of 1908, he expresses his wish to be a saint. By being a saint Price meant that he should belong to both Jesus and the Blessed Mother.[46] In 1909 Fred stated in a letter to the Blessed Mother that he wanted to be a saint: "But in all and above all, my Mother, I wish to be a *saint*—that is, that I should belong to our Love [Jesus] and be of Him and in Him and all His entirely. O my own loved Mother, help me to this—that I may this year be a saint!—*unknown buried in Him* and *your love*, Mother. Again and again I wish this, Mother."[47]

In October 1909 his concept of how one is a saint changed after he read a pamphlet summarizing Brother Lawrence's experience of the presence of God.[48] It moved his understanding from *one living in Jesus* to *Jesus living in the individual.* In 1911, on the twenty-fifth anniversary of Fred's ordination to the priesthood, while he and James A. Walsh were seeking approval to establish their foreign mission seminary, he writes: "I have gone over the various years and one desire stands out now that it is all over—that I have not lived, Mother, His life. "I live now not I" but our Love [Jesus]. I will say Mass tomorrow the 25th anniversary and it will be for that—that the little of what remains to me of my misspent life will be given to Him—I shall not live but He shall live in me."[49] This change of focus set the stage for what he would term "the miracle" at Lourdes and for rejection of the Ignatian Exercises.

Beginnings of the Foreign Mission Seminary (1910–1911)

The concept of a foreign mission seminary developed over many years. Father Price was encouraged at the Washington Conference of 1904 where he met Fr. James Anthony Walsh. By May 1909 the concept of foreign missionary activity led to a statement that appeared in the "Notes & Remarks" section of *Truth:*

> Another great need of this country—we might say its greatest need—is a Foreign Mission Seminary with its preparatory adjuncts. What we need in this country—above every other country—is the cultivation of a spirit of sacrifice for our faith, and nothing will so reach the root of the matter as a Foreign Mission Seminary with all that means. In seminaries the very flower of Catholic faith is cultivated—the giving of our life—our absolute martyrdom (for that is what it means) for the spread of our faith for foreign missions. Such a seminary ought to be established in Washington around the Catholic University, and it ought to have preparatory schools in all our large Catholic centers—in New York, in Boston, in Philadelphia, in Chicago, in St. Louis, in San Francisco.[50]

Upon reading this passage in *Truth,* Walsh sent a letter to Price thanking him for his accurate assessment of the situation and expressing the fact that the idea of a foreign mission seminary was also close to his heart.[51]

In 1910 Father Price was ready to move toward establishing this seminary. It was Fred Price who sought out James Walsh at the 1910 Eucharistic Congress in Montreal to discuss the possibilities of the seminary. After hours of discussion and several letters, Price was in Cardinal Gibbon's office asking for support for the new project; he visited several bishops to enlist their support.

Fred Price's personal visits to his long-standing and numerous connections with the hierarchy and ability to explain the vision of a foreign mission seminary were the main forces behind the bishops' support for this seminary. That support launched Price and Walsh on a successful trip to look at the English Foreign Mission Seminary at Mill Hill and the Paris Foreign Mission Seminary and to visit Rome and the Vatican.[52]

Notes

1. *Diary*, 5.
2. *Diary*, 10.
3. *Diary*, 613.
4. *Diary*, 6–9.
5. Patrick J. Byrne, *Father Price*, 32.
6. *Diary*, 4.
7. Robert E. Sheridan, ed., *A Symposium*, 105.
8. John C. Murrett, *Tarheel*, 57–8.
9. Robert E. Sheridan, ed., *A Symposium*, 52.
10. Robert E. Sheridan, ed., *A Symposium*, 113.
11. Thomas Frederick Price, *Collected Letters of Thomas Frederick Price, M.M., 1883-1919* Robert E. Sheridan, ed. (Maryknoll, N.Y.: Maryknoll Fathers, 1981) 18–27.
12. *Diary*, 311.
13. *Diary*, 513.
14. For the Sulpician method, see chapter 5. The Church in Maryland has been influenced by the Jesuits since the founding of the colony. See Robert Emmett Curran, *American Jesuit Spirituality* (New York: Paulist, 1988) 171–2.
15. *Diary*, 206, 239, 312, 319, 416, 423.
16. *Diary*, 47, 87, 162, 283.
17. *Diary*, 87.
18. *Diary*, 10, 87, 148, 341.

19. *Diary,* 341, 349, 350.

20. George C. Powers, *Biography,* 54.

21. John C. Murrett, *Tarheel,* 29.

22. Robert E. Sheridan, ed., *A Symposium,* 207.

23. *Diary,* 2503–4.

24. Robert E. Sheridan, ed., *A Symposium,* 51, 104.

25. Evelyn Underhill, *Mysticism,* 169.

26. Ignatius of Loyola, *The Spiritual Exercises of St. Ignatius of Loyola,* trans. Lewis Delmage (Boston: Daughters of St. Paul, 1978) 57.

27. Patrick J. Byrne, *Father Price,* 22–3.

28. John C. Murrett, *Tarheel,* 74.

29. *Diary,* 2932.

30. *Diary,* 2940–4.

31. John C. Murrett, *Tarheel,* 215.

32. *Diary,* 241.

33. *Diary,* 242.

34. *Diary,* 202.

35. Edward T. Gilbert letter to Vincent S. Waters, February 20, 1952, *Collected Letters,* 385.

36. John C. Murrett, *Tarheel,* 33.

37. *Diary,* 87.

38. *Diary,* 7–12.

39. John C. Murrett, *Tarheel,* 76.

40. *Diary,* 312.

41. *Diary,* 200, 510.

42. *Diary,* 311.

43. *Diary,* 10, 87, 148, 341.

44. *Diary,* 341, 349, 350.

45. *Diary,* 178, 206.

46. *Diary,* 39, 126–8, 269.

47. *Diary,* 87.

48. *Diary,* 197.

49. *Diary,* 508–9.

50. *Truth,* 13:5 (May 1909) 131–2.

51. John C. Murrett, *Tarheel,* 78.

52. John C. Murrett, *Tarheel,* 100–9.

7

The Groom:
Theological Proclamation

Unfortunately there is no book by Father Price that could be titled *A Consolidated Personal Theology, A Summary of Christian Doctrine* or any other systematic theological tract. There are no indications that Fred ever intended to write such a book. However, for this study we need to construct a consolidated, expressive theological study that will provide the archetypical statements needed for a comparison with his experiential theology.

Fortunately Fred wanted to express his theology to his fellow North Carolinians. He did this through apologetic material in *Truth* magazine. Since *Truth* was not a systematic presentation of his theology, Fred's expressive theology was supplemented by the catechism that Fred used as a text in the seminary, namely, Deharbe's *A Complete Catechism of the Catholic Religion*,[1] and which he recommended to the readers of *Truth*.[2]

In constructing his expressive theological archetypes, we must remember that Fred Price's audience, being non-Catholic, was concerned about the Catholic belief in Jesus, the Bible, and the devotion to the saints, especially Mary. Price's theological background was certainly Roman Catholic, but it was a Catholicism that was immersed in an anti-Roman Catholic environment. Knowledge and defense of Catholic beliefs in this environment was important.

Faith

Fred's operational concept of faith prior to and during his North Carolina ministry is important to our understanding of his theological growth. As editor of *Truth,* Fred used John Cardinal Newman's understanding of faith several times as the frontispiece for the magazine: "It [faith] is assenting to doctrine as true, which we do not see, which we cannot prove, because God says it is true, who cannot lie. This is what faith was at the time of the Apostles, . . . it must be now."[3] The foundation of faith that Fred was using at this time was faith in Church doctrine. This type of faith is what some Thomistic scholars call pseudo-faith or faith in statements.[4]

During these first four stages of Fred's life, church doctrine and teachings were the code or standard that he not only applied to his own life but believed that if his fellow Tarheels could know the true teaching of the Church, they would become Catholics.

Trinity

The doctrine of the Trinity was not a point of contention between Tarheel Protestants and Church teaching. Both groups used the Trinity as a starting point for doctrinal discussion. It was the key assumption underlying the presentation of the Catholic Christology in *Truth*.

The Deharbe catechism emphasized that the doctrine of the Trinity is critical to the Christian faith and that it was a mystery that cannot be understood because of our own limitations but which we can understand through faith.[5]

The trinitarian understanding starts with the concept that God is eternal and a pure spirit.

> God is a spirit, and therefore is the Divine Substance. There are no parts no divisions. . . .
>
> By faith we learn that God also exists in the Unity of One Substance, and that in this One, Simple Divine Substance there exists a Trinity . . . . a Trinity of Persons.
>
> As God is infinite, there could never be a time when He was less than He is, nor when He should become more than He was. What ever is in God, is in Him, therefore, eternally, and the priority of Persons cannot be a priority of time or age.[6]

The acceptance of God as spirit leads to the conclusion that God has neither divisions nor material substances and therefore God has neither parts nor can God be divided in any way.[7]

Christology

Fred Price's Christology has two focal points which were the areas of concern to his missionary audience. First is the divinity of the Savior expressed in the title "Son of God," and there is the divinity and humanity as the real presence of Christ in the Eucharist. Between these two points there is a systematic chain of christological understanding from the second person of the Blessed Trinity, to the Son of God, to the Son of Man, to the real presence of Christ in the Eucharist.

The belief in the divinity of Jesus Christ is basic to Catholicism. The literal meaning of "Son of God" is taken from Scripture and is one of the self-proclamations of Jesus as God. Since he is the Son of God, Jesus Christ is the Second Person of the Blessed Trinity, the Son. The christological understanding is firmly linked with the trinitarian concepts.[8]

In accepting that Christ is divine and the Second Person of the Trinity, it follows that he is "everywhere though invisible."[9] Christ is the eternal Son of the Father and in becoming flesh he is the channel of communication, the "Word."[10] The second person of the Trinity becoming man is a redeeming action. Jesus Christ, the God-man, has a divine nature, which in unity with the human nature yields a personal oneness. As God he is everywhere, as man he is only found at the right hand of the Father and in the Eucharist.[11]

Fred proclaimed and supported the Council of Trent concerning Christ in the Eucharist being whole and entire under both species, body, blood, soul and divinity under the form of bread and wine. The distinction between Roman Catholic and Protestant views was critically important to Fred's ministry. In commenting on how the humanity of Jesus in the Eucharist can be in so many churches at one time, Fred wrote: "We don't pretend to explain it. We know that it is true because Christ has said it and Him we believe and trust."[12]

The Saints

The devotions, statues and prayers of petition to the saints in popular Roman Catholic piety were major problems for the

Protestants who thought that the Catholics were worshiping the saints as divine beings. Fred uses both the individual and corporate link in and through Jesus Christ called the Communion of Saints as the theological understanding behind the popular practices. The saints in heaven form an important link in the dialogue between God and the faithful on earth. Statues and pictures remind us of the saints in heaven as well as Jesus. Originally veneration of the saints developed as a response to the miracles at their tombs in the early Church. Praying to God is praising, thanking, begging, or meditation. Dialogue is with the saints who are close to God and can intercede for those on earth.[13] Fred knew that there were superstitions and abuses by the faithful with regard to devotions to saints in heaven.[14] For his Protestant readership Fred compared this dialogue between the saints on earth and the saints in heaven to the practice of asking a friend to pray for them.[15] He noted that there is a special place among the saints reserved for the Blessed Mother.

Role of the Blessed Mother

If the Catholic attitude towards saints and their statues bothered the Protestants, the devotion to the Blessed Mother was even more upsetting to Fred's fellow Tarheels. The issues included the divinity of Mary, the meaning of the "Immaculate Conception," and the title "Mother of God."

Fred's expressive theology of the Blessed Mother flows from biblical accounts and creedal statements. Mary's being a virgin and Jesus being conceived by her by the power of the Holy Ghost and not by a human father is critical to the doctrinal position that Jesus Christ is the God-man. Mary then is the source of the human nature of the God-man and the Holy Ghost is the source of the divine nature. Mary always remained a Virgin incomparably pure and undefiled. Various articles in *Truth* noted that the perpetual virginity of Mary had been proclaimed since early times[16] and that she was conceived without original sin. "Original sin is that guilt and stain of sin which we inherit from Adam, who was the origin and head of mankind, and the sin committed by Adam was the sin of disobedience when he ate the forbidden fruit, and not sexual intercourse."[17] Mary is the closest to God.[18]

In *Truth* he explains devotion to the Blessed Mother by quoting Father Faber:

> The devotion to the Blessed Virgin is true imitation of Jesus; for next to the glory of His Father, it was the devotion nearest and dearest to His Sacred Heart. It is a peculiarly solid devotion because it is perpetually occupied with the hatred of sin and acquisition of virtue. To neglect it is to despise God, for she is His ordinance; and to wound Jesus, because she is His Mother. God Himself has placed her in the Church as a distinct power; and hence she is operative, and a fountain of miracles, and a part of religion which we can in nowise put in abeyance.[19]

In terms of Southern society, the Blessed Mother is in the perfect position to be seen as the kinkeeper, the moral arbiter and guide for a family or an individual.

Bernadette

Within Fred's personal life and understanding of the Blessed Mother, a girl from the Pyrenees town of Lourdes was very important. The appearances of the Blessed Mother to Bernadette Soubirous in 1858 not only reinforced the increasing Catholic devotion to Mary but also confirmed the doctrinal understanding of the Immaculate Conception. Upon her death in 1879, she was buried in the crypt of her convent in Nevers, France.

Fred obviously believed that Bernadette was one of the saints in heaven from their first mystical meeting in 1911. In her 1918 biography he stated that one of the reasons for publishing an English-language version her life story in 1914 was to "forward the process of her canonization."[20] He further claimed that Bernadette was a child of the Immaculate Conception and that Bernadette was the blessed Mother's personal confidante; in fact, a copy of her: "[Bernadette is] purest, humblest and most crucified virgin and victim, when the Immaculate Conception chose her out of all the earth to be her own most dear and predestined child to whom she promised heaven. . . .[21]

Bernadette as one of the saints in heaven is someone with whom those on earth can dialogue as a confidante of the Blessed Mother and one in Eucharistic union with Christ.

Marriage as Sacrament

To evaluate Fred's experiential theology it is helpful to discuss his expressional theology of marriage and the role of women within the Christian context. The grace that sanctifies a married couple in union with Christ helps each party love and be faithful to each other—to love each other as Christ loved the Church, to lead a holy life, to bring up children in the love and fear of God, to fulfill the duties of married life, to bear difficulties.[22]

Celibacy of Priests

A point of great curiosity to Protestants and southern culture of Fred's time was the issue of celibacy for Roman Catholic priests. Fred would answer by stating that priests do not marry because both the Lord and St. Paul stated that celibacy was a higher state than marriage. Therefore the Church commands that her clergy be of the higher state. There was, furthermore, the understanding that a priest might better love all of those entrusted to him as his children and entirely serve them.[23]

Understanding of Women

Women had a definite position in Fred's understanding that was as firm as his understanding concerning celibate clergy. In 1907 he mentioned in *Truth* that the Protestant practice of "handing over pulpits to women was one sign of unfaithfulness.[24] This reaction had a cultural side as well as a doctrinal one. Southern women were seen as keepers and managers of the house and did not conduct business outside the home.

Women were to be thought of as something sacred to men, but at the same time they were to be made holy by men. Woman makes man strong, and it is his role to defend her. This position was very close to the understanding of southern chivalry, and the lady of the castle, in which the man defended her and, in the process, received meaning and purpose. Continuing this line of thought, women were considered to be the weaker sex. When a woman erred it was unfortunate but, of course, when a man went wrong it was far worse. Clearly, responsibility rested with the male. Curiously, however, there is a protest by Fred in *Truth* against the poor state of some women going to work for a small wage or of their being treated as a "single servant kept at home."[25]

In an article entitled "The Position of Women in the Catholic Church," Fred noted the agitation for women's rights in Protestant countries. The article maintained that Catholics offer women the freedom of expression for their talents and state of life in religious orders. Fred also clarified that the Church proclaims the dignity of motherhood, the defense of virtue, and the inviolate sacredness of marriage. As well as being a foundational part of southern culture, this understanding is based on the special position of Mary as mother in his expressive theology:

> Let every womanly heart whatever its religion may be, that is rejoiced by the chivalrous love of a good man, let every happy home where the mother is recognized as the father's beloved and equal partner, and where the beautiful spirit of family unity reigns undisturbed—let all there arise and honor the woman all generations shall call blessed, and let them, with united voice give grateful praise to that Church which, in proclaiming Mary's dignity exalted Mary's sex and which in preserving inviolate and indissoluble the bonds of marriage, has made possible woman's advancement in the past and has made safe for her the pathway to the full exercise of her every right and power in the future.[26]

Fred claims that because of the positive stand of the Catholic Church on women, Protestant feminists are converting to Roman Catholicism.[27]

Certainly Fred had a chivalrous view of women with the sisterhood being the best expression of both dedication to God and personal development. The purity and holiness and position of women was very important to Fred.

Sexuality and Sensuality

In Fred's theological context "temptation" is a technical term. It specifically applies to the sins against the sixth and ninth commandments, "Thou shall not commit adultery" and "Thou shall not covet thy neighbor's wife." Sins against these commandments range from adultery to drunkenness and revelry that might lead to impure thoughts and desires. The scope of temptations include not only unchaste looks, words, jests and touches, but also violations of modesty or things that lead to impurity. It is important, therefore, to protect oneself from curious eyes, immodest dress, flatterers (seducers), obscene materials, and indecent entertainment.

Papal Teaching

Faith for Fred was the acceptance of the doctrine of the Church as true. It is true even if we cannot see or prove it because God said it was true. In *Truth* Fred openly attacked Modernism in 1907 and published Pope Pius X's *Syllabus of July 3, 1907*.[28] He emphasized that private revelation is improper; we must rely on Church authority. To properly hold to these doctrine we must seek the protection of the Blessed Mother.[29] We can trust in the Church for "the Church is the pillar and ground of truth. The Holy Spirit is to remain with her forever to teach her all the truth."[30]

It appears that Fred did not have an innovative theology and was not involved in theological research. His expressive theology was nicely complemented by the theology that he was taught at the seminary, and he had a burning desire to accurately proclaim and live the doctrine of the Church in his ministry. For example, when Fred was challenged as to whether or not his Marian devotion was an acceptable form of prayer, in response he made every effort to understand and apply the doctrine correctly.

Notes

1. Joseph Deharbe, *A Complete Catechism of the Catholic Religion,* John Flander, trans. (New York: Schartz, Kirwin, 1912, 6th ed.).
2. Deharbe's catechism was strongly recommended by Father Price to the readers of *Truth* as late as July 1911, (15:7) 213.
3. John Cardinal Newman, "What is Faith," *Truth* 5:8 (November 1900) frontispiece.
4. For a discussion of faith within this context, see Carlos Cirne-Lima, *Personal Faith* (New York: Herder and Herder New York, 1965). See also Martin Buber, *Two Types of Faith* (New York: Macmillian, 1951).
5. Deharbe, *Catechism,* 94.
6. T. F. Price, "Question Box," *Truth* 11:5 (September 1907) 125.
7. "He [God] has but one nature, yet three Persons in Him. The unity refers to the nature, and the Trinity to the Persons (Deharbe, *Catechism,* 94). For Father Price the human faculties are only an example

of a trinity and have no relationship to the Trinity which we know through faith, "Question Box," *Truth* 11:5 (September 1907) 125.

8. Joseph Deharbe, *Catechism,* 111–4.

9. T. F. Price, "Question Box," *Truth,* 11:3 (July 1907) 79.

10. T. F. Price, "Question Box," *Truth* 11:4 (August 1907) 96.

11. T. F. Price, "Question Box," *Truth* 11:13 (July 1907) 66; "Question Box," *Truth* 10:7 (November 1906) 216.

12. T. F. Price, "Question Box," *Truth* 15:11 November 1911) 337.

13. T. F. Price, "Question Box," *Truth* 11:13 (September 1901) 212.

14. T. F. Price, "Question Box," *Truth* 3:10 (January 1900) 332–3.

15. T. F. Price, "Question Box," *Truth* 4:9 (December 1900) 306.

16. T. F. Price, "Question Box," *Truth* 4:3 (June 1900) 91; "Question Box," *Truth* 4:11 (February 1901) 372.

17. T. F. Price, "Question Box," *Truth* 13:1 (February 1909) 52.

18. T. F. Price, "Question Box," *Truth* (December 1906) 245–6.

19. *Truth* 5:5 (August 1901) 156.

20. T. F. Price, ed., *The Lily of Mary: Bernadette of Lourdes* (New York: The Bureau of the Immaculate Conception, 1918) 17.

21. Thomas Frederick Price, ed., *Bernadette of Lourdes* (New York: Devin-Adair, 1914) 11.

22. T. F. Price, "Question Box," *Truth* 14:11 (November 1910) 349–50; Deharbe's *Catechism* (pp. 304–6) has a similar list of duties except in "d," which states that the husband should treat his wife with kindness, and she should obey him in all that is honorable and to manage the domestic concerns.

23. T. F. Price, "Notes and Remarks," *Truth* 13:7 (July 1909) 180–1.

24. T. F. Price, "Question Box," *Truth* 10:9 (January 1907) 282.

25. Fr. Vaughan, S.J., "On Women," *Truth* 15:12 (December 1911) 378–9.

26. T. F. Price, "The Positions of Women in the Catholic Church," *Truth* 10:1 (May 1906) 9.

27. Fr. Sailiere, "Feminism," originally published as "The Reaction Against Feminism in Germany." *Revue de Deux Mondes* trans. in *The Living Age,* with introduction by T. F. Price, *Truth* 4:7 (October 1900) 213–6.

28. Pius X, "Decree of Holy Roman and Universal Inquisition, Wednesday July 3, 1907," with introduction "The New Syllabus" by T. F. Price, *Truth* 11:5 (September 1907) 114–7.

29. T. F. Price, "Question Box," *Truth* 11:7 (December 1907) 205–7.

30. J. S. Vaughan, "Thoughts for All Times," *Truth* 11:8 (December 1907) frontispiece.

8

The Bride: Bernadette Soubirous (1844–1879)*

Marie Bernard (Bernadette) was born January 7, 1844 to François Soubirous and Louise Casterot in Lourdes, a Pyrenees village in southern France. By July that year Louise was pregnant with their second child and Bernadette was given to Marie Lagues Aravant to be nursed. The Aravants lived two miles away in Bartrès. The baby girl returned to her family in October 1845.[1]

Business did not go well for the Soubirous, and by the winter of 1855 they lost their mill and house. Bernadette suffered from asthma and at times was faint from suffocation. At eleven she was sent to live with her god-mother and aunt Bernarde in Bartrès for seven to eight months. She treated Bernadette as one of her own.[2]

In 1857 Marie Aravant asked if Bernadette could come to live with them and help watch over the younger children. However, she was given the job of shepherding the lambs. Mr. Aravant was a harsh man, and the neighbors would supplement the food she was given. The stories by others and by Bernadette herself concerning her childhood indicate that she was naive, a slow learner, and illiterate. At age fourteen she returned to Lourdes and again lived with her family.[3]

*This chapter is based on the two biographies that Fred Price edited, *Bernadette of Lourdes* (1914) and *The Lily of Mary* (1918).

The Apparitions

During the winter of 1858, Bernadette, her sister Toinette, and a girl friend were searching for firewood in the Massabieille cave area above the mill near the Gave River. At a grotto she was separated from the others as they crossed the millrace. While taking off her shoes to cross the river, she heard a wind and then looking up into the grotto saw a lady. Her response was to try to say the Rosary, but she could not make the Sign of the Cross to start the prayers. The Lady, as Bernadette called her, began to make the Sign of the Cross, and then Bernadette was able to pray. Shortly, the Lady disappeared. On the way home Bernadette realized that the others had seen nothing. This was the first of eighteen apparitions that Bernadette witnessed between February 11 and July 16 of that year.[4]

The following is a summary of the apparitions that occurred after this first meeting:[5]

2nd—February 14,
The Sunday following the first apparition, Bernadette and six friends were allowed to go back to the grotto and began to pray the Rosary. The Lady appeared and to witnesses Bernadette's face was transformed (the beginning of the ecstatic experiences).

3rd—February 18,
At the third apparition Bernadette offered the Lady a pen and paper. She said that it is not necessary that it be put in writing. One of the other parts of the dialogue was a request to Bernadette, "Would you have the kindness to come here for fifteen days!" Another was for Bernadette personally, "I do not promise you that you will be happy in this world but in the other."

4th—February 19,
Bernadette spoke of voices saying "Escape, escape," but the Lady's gaze in their direction silenced them.

5th—February 21,
The Lady taught Bernadette her own prayer.

6th—February 22,
Dr. Dozones, a physician, observed her during the vision. The Lady tells Bernadette to "pray for sinners."

7th—February 23,

Bernadette is told she cannot reveal this conversation to others. "I forbid you to tell this to anyone."

8th—February 24,

In a second reference to sinners, the Lady tells Bernadette, "Penitence, Penitence, Penitence."

9th—February 25,

"Go to the spring and drink and wash there" (the source of the famous healing waters of Lourdes). Healing within the Hebrew and Christian traditions has long indicated the presence of God or someone sent from God (Exod 23:25, Pss 4, 16, 22, 23, 38, 39, 42, 43, 102, 30, 31, 103, 116; the numerous healings by Jesus in the Gospels; the disciples' healings: Luke 10:1-20, Acts 3:1-10).

10th—February 26,

Again there is a reference to sinners when the Lady gives a command to Bernadette. "Kiss the earth for sinners." Bernadette complies. (This is the third reference to sinners by the Lady).

11th—February 27,

Bernadette is told, "Go tell the priest that a chapel should be built here."

12th—February 28,

Two thousand people came to watch. The girl and the Lady have a private conversation.

13th—March 1,

The Lady knew that Bernadette had a different Rosary in her pocket.

14th—March 2,

Repeating the previous command for the priest to build a chapel, the Lady added: "I desire that the people should come in procession." Upon telling the priest of the Lady's request, he demanded that she request a sign from the Lady.

March 3,

Bernadette visited the grotto and prayed but there was no apparition, and she did not experience her usual ecstasy (This non-apparition is an apparition in the negative sense in that it is a response to the demand for a sign by the priest. From the biblical perspective, asking for such signs especially by church authorities is not recommended [Mark 8:11-12, Matt 16:1-4]. Within the Hebrew/biblical understanding, silence should not be surprising or considered out of place).

15th—March 4,

Twenty thousand people came to watch. Bernadette was in an ecstatic state for over an hour.

Three weeks of prayer at the grotto followed without an appearance of the Lady to Bernadette.

16th—March 25,

Bernadette asks the Lady her name three times. The Lady replies, "I am the Immaculate Conception" (The response after the third request is very Hebrew/biblical. The third asking indicates sincerity and truth of a statement).

17th—April 7,

During ecstasy Bernadette's left hand was not burned by the flame of the candle she held under it with her right hand for fifteen minutes (Dr. Dozones was present and examined her).

On June 3 Bernadette received Holy Communion for the first time.

18th—July 16,

Just after receiving Communion at Mass, she raced to the grotto, which had been fenced off. Over the fencing Bernadette saw the Lady for the last time.

Certainly the Lady cared for Bernadette and was present to her. Also the Lady encouraged Bernadette to be concerned for others. Additionally there were the physical manifestations of transcendent experiences in the trance-like ecstasies and the healing spring water.

These grotto events in Bernadette's life were not without their own hassles and problems. During the early apparitions her way was blocked by the police. Realizing that the grotto, the rose bush, and the spring might be important relics, the civil and church authorities moved to protect the area. Her story was initially not accepted by the Church, which launched a four-year investigation. In January 1862 Bishop Lawrence of Tarbes declared that the apparitions had really happened. The priest did not receive the command to build a chapel positively, at first. After diocesan approval of the visions and several miracles were claimed, a statue that did not look like the vision was erected at the grotto. Finally, in May 1866 the crypt of the basilica was dedicated. The press was extremely skeptical. The crowds visiting Lourdes tore at Bernadette's clothes for souvenirs.[6]

After the crowds and investigations, Bernadette joined the Sisters of Charity and Christian Instruction at Nevers, France. Upon receiving her habit she spent the rest of her life in the cloister. She had a sense of humility, knowing that God chooses the least.[7]

She obediently prayed for sinners and accepted her suffering from asthma with its convulsions, hemorrhaging, and lung trouble, and the pain of an abscessed knee. Through the pain she shared in Jesus' crucifixion. In that context the Eucharist, both received and venerated in the tabernacle, was important to Bernadette. She sought unity with Christ through poverty and purity. Bernadette herself proclaimed the intimacy of the union: "I place my joy in being a victim of the heart of Jesus; union, intimate union with Him, such as St. John had, by purity and love."[8] Her Eucharistic life is described as "a hidden life, a life of annihilation, carried out in silence, prayer and renunciation."[9]

Bernadette died at age thirty-six on April 16, 1879 at the convent in Nevers. Four days after her death, her body was reported to still be limp and her skin the same color as the day she died. With great ceremony she was buried in the convent crypt.[10] Her first biography *Bernadette of Lourdes* was written in support of Bernadette's canonization. It contains numerous stories of answers to prayers that were said at her tomb from the time of her death in 1879 through 1908.[11]

Notes

1. T. F. Price, ed., *Bernadette of Lourdes,* trans. J. H. Gregory (New York: Devin-Adair, 1914) 39–40.

2. T. F. Price, ed., *Bernadette of Lourdes,* 40–1.

3. T. F. Price, ed., *Bernadette of Lourdes,* 42–6.

4. T. F. Price, ed., *Bernadette of Lourdes,* 46–9.

5. T. F. Price, ed., *Bernadette of Lourdes,* 49–72.

6. Thomas Frederick Price, ed., *The Lily of Mary: Bernadette of Lourdes* (New York: Bureau of the Immaculate Conception, 1918) 56–63.

7. T. F. Price, ed., *The Lily of Mary,* 70–1.

8. T. F. Price, ed., *The Lily of Mary,* 75.

9. T. F. Price, ed., *The Lily of Mary,* 78–9.

10. T. F. Price, ed., *Bernadette of Lourdes,* 244–6.

11. T. F. Price, ed., *Bernadette of Lourdes,* 247–60.

9

Backdrop to the Marriage
(1911–1919)

The meeting, friendship, courtship, and marriage of the American priest and French nun is played out with a sweeping worldwide backdrop. The scenes change from Lourdes and Nevers, France, to North Carolina and New York, and it includes travels throughout the Northeast and Midwest, as well as to Canada for pilgrimages to the Shrine of St. Anne de Beaupré near Quebec City and then finally to China.

Upon completion of the work in Rome, Fred wanted to make a thirty-day Ignatian retreat in Dublin, Ireland. On the way from Rome to Dublin, he detoured through Lourdes, France, to visit the shrine where the Blessed Mother had appeared to Bernadette.

At the end of his initial short visit he reported that he "spent from 12 o'clock last night till 8 or 9 this morning praying at the grotto and all my difficulties seemed to disappear and you granted or seemed to grant me some great favors. . . . In one sense I never felt so much happiness."[1]

As scheduled, Fred proceeded to Dublin where due to a communication/scheduling problem, he did not make his retreat. Again the *Diary* indicates how much the visit at Lourdes had affected him: "My own loved Mother, I seem to feel your grace and favor in this upheaval with the Jesuits. At Lourdes I seemed to feel most keenly the necessity of dropping everything else— methods, plans and have none except what you should develop, only praying and doing penance for sinners as Bernadette was told and then engaging in what should develop."[2] From the July day on which the above was written, the spiritual exercises of St. Ignatius became far less important to Fred's spirituality.

When he returned to Lourdes, Fred was impressed by the dedication of Bernadette to the Blessed Mother and her announcement as the Immaculate Conception. It is at this time that he met the Soubirous Family and began an ever-deepening relationship with them; he even received a cloak from Jean Marie Soubirous, Bernadette's brother.[3] After forty-one days at Lourdes, he traveled to Nevers, France, where Bernadette is buried. The mother superior of the convent granted his request for a prayer vigil in the crypt with Bernadette. This was the beginning of a life-long relationship with the convent.

Both the Soubirous family and the sisters in Nevers took Fred Price seriously and were supportive of his work concerning Bernadette and the Blessed Mother. The sisters understood the deep relationship between the Tarheel and Bernadette. For seventy years the sisters kept his correspondence confidential. The support of the family and the sisters points to Fred's sincerity towards Bernadette and acceptance of the spirituality.

The second and longer visit to Lourdes and the stop at Nevers produced plans for a Society of the Immaculate Conception with headquarters at Lourdes and a magazine. The objective of this organization was to bring the message of Lourdes to the United States.[4] Fred also had a growing sense of being Bernadette's spiritual brother and of being dedicated to her.

From his first visit to Lourdes, he admired Bernadette's simple life of unselfish dedication.[5] As he left Europe on the SS Winifredian, he made a "resolution . . . to call myself by your sweet name whenever that was possible as my Sister—Bernadette—Mary Bernard." He began in that very letter to sign it: "M.B.N. of Jesus" (Mary Bernadette Nazareth of Jesus).[6] Following the practice of some religious orders and with his taking the name Mary Bernard, he began to ask others to address him as "Father Bernadette."

Maryknoll (1911–1917)

Upon return to the United States the co-founders of the new Catholic Foreign Mission Society set about disentangling themselves from their previous ministries in Nazareth and Boston. Fred had considerably more entanglements than James Anthony Walsh. In fact, it was January 1912 before Fred changed the signature on the daily letters in the *Diary* from "Mary Bernadette N.[azareth] of Jesus" to "Mary Bernadette" (This indicates a giving up of place that was so important to Fred Price, as it was to other southerners. This is not only a change of internal understanding but also a significant re-orientation for Fred Price).[7]

Shortly after he joined Father Walsh at Hawthorne, New York, the current site of the Catholic Foreign Mission Society of America was purchased in Ossining on a hill over-looking the Hudson Valley. The name "Maryknoll" had already been chosen with the joyful concurrence of Father Bernadette. For most of the time between 1912 and 1918 Fred was out promoting the new society. He also was spiritual director at Maryknoll Seminary and headed the preparatory seminary in Scranton, the Venard.

He traveled from diocese to diocese, parish to parish, preaching and passing out the envelopes and pencils to the parishioners in the pews (an idea developed by Fred), getting subscriptions to *Field Afar* and donations.

During his time as spiritual director at Maryknoll, he made a significant impression on the students, who have commented on his piety and devotion to prayer and the Blessed Mother and love of Bernadette; they also attested to his firmness during spiritual direction.[8]

Venard and Healing

Fred worked to establish a minor seminary in Scranton that was named after Theophane Venard, and on one occasion he was the school's director. The preparatory school opened in the fall 1913, and Fred replaced the ill Fr. John I. Lane as director until January 1914 when Fr. John McCabe from Mill Hill, England, arrived to assume the post.

On December 24, 1913, Fred saw an oculist for an ulcer in his left eye. The condition was so bad that there was a danger of total blindness. Fred prayed intensely to Blessed Theophane Venard for a cure. A relic of Theophane was applied to the eye and it was kept near him that night. The eye improved rapidly.[9]

Publishing

In 1914 Fred edited and had published an English translation of Bernadette Soubirous' life entitled *Bernadette of Lourdes*.[10] He also established the Bureau of the Immaculate Conception in New York City. This organization was interested in proclaiming the message of Lourdes to America. Fred eventually (1918) published a shorter biography of Bernadette through the bureau called *The Lily of Mary: Bernadette of Lourdes*.[11]

Pilgrimages

In addition to the most important first pilgrimage to Lourdes in 1911, Father Bernadette also made pilgrimages to Lourdes and Nevers in 1912 and 1913. Due to tensions in Europe and then World War I, the pilgrimages made in the following years were to St. Anne de Beaupré in Canada. Each of these pilgrimages deepened the relationship between Fred, the Blessed Mother, and Bernadette.

Struggles

Fred experienced three major problems during the Maryknoll years. They were the inner struggle to become a saint, the struggle to do the work that he thought he should be doing, and the coming to grips with the life he had to leave behind in taking on the foreign mission seminary project.

First, he gave up Nazareth and his personal dedication to making every Tarheel a Roman Catholic. Along with that there was the rejection of placing the missionary seminary in North Carolina and the need to change his own thinking from working as a missionary first in North Carolina and then across the rest of the United States and finally in foreign lands. If this was not enough, he also turned over the publication of *Truth* to the International Truth Society in Brooklyn, New York. The pain involved in these losses was on many levels.

The time and effort that had gone into making an idea a reality and seeing dreams limited or changed caused frustration; along with this there was the grieving experienced in any loss.

While Fred saw the need for the loss, it was still there. The new dedication to Bernadette's work continued to cause a divergence between missionary action and the missionary call. These tensions were added to his inner struggle for saintliness.

Two inner struggles constantly reoccurred with Fred; both due to his humanity. The first is mentioned throughout the *Diary*, i.e., Fred struggled with temptations that paralleled his anger over the increasingly immodest dress of even "good Catholic women." Wanting to be a saint, rid himself of vileness, and later be worthy of his spouse, he dedicated himself to purity using prayer to assist him; at times, even the lash was used for mortification. He also added the physical pain for ill health to his list of purgative sufferings.

The other struggle going on within Fred was that of combating pride. The early pages of the *Diary* speak of how "he," Fred Price, would convert North Carolina and are filled with plans for his society. Later through prayer he realized how much pride dominated his life. Often he accepted humiliation as good for him, such as traveling steerage to Europe or only wearing donated clothing. Humiliation brought him closer to true poverty.

Unlike the merging of the spiritual relationships that occurred after Lourdes, his avenues of vision and available roads to do missionary work diverged. Shortly after receiving the Vatican approval of the new society, he was drawing up plans for another organization to spread the message of Lourdes. Fred also wanted to establish a mission seminary in the United States. He even begged for money to support himself personally. He appeared to be a man pulled in three directions: the original vision of home missions with a seminary, spending all his effort in carrying out the work of Bernadette and proclaiming the Immaculate Conception, and going forward with the foreign mission project. The conflict produces years of constant turmoil in action and prayer, but poverty for Fred Price was a badge of honor for the Blessed Mother and brought him closer to his beloved.

All of these struggles created problems for Fr. James Anthony Walsh. For example, Fred would not let his name or picture be used in *Field Afar*. After one issue did contain his picture, he wrote the following letter to James Anthony on April 23, 1916:

My Dear Fr. Walsh,

I have been given to understand that you have published a picture of me in the F.A. This matter has pained me deeply. I trust you will see your way to give me the assurance that all plates and negatives concerning the picture in question will be immediately destroyed and I trust that you will not allow the matter to happen again. Otherwise I fear that the freedom of our future intercourse will be marred.

> Respectfully and sincerely,
> Your humble servant,
>
> Thos. F. Price[12]

Fred's dedication to a broader scope of mission than just the Far East moved him to write to James Anthony in 1916 concerning his leaving Maryknoll:

It seems to me that I should make to them [the Directors of Maryknoll] the statement of my own position—substantially as follows: I wish to state that as the Maryknoll work is confined to Pagans in Pagan lands and since there are many other missions such as the Philippines, Porto Rica *[sic.]*, South American Countries, and some districts in the U.S.A., etc., which are in great need of American missionaries, I have been encouraged by Ecclesiastics of weight and authority to attempt as soon as my presence is not necessary to the Maryknoll work the foundation of a work to supply the needs of such missions. . . .[13]

The seriousness of this letter should not be underestimated. The *Diary* records plans for an American mission and Fred's leaving Maryknoll.[14] It was only a last-minute intervention by James A. Walsh and Cardinal Farley of New York that stopped the new seminary's foundation at Emmitsburg, Maryland.

It was through prayer that Fred's tension over which mission work to pursue was slowly resolved. In 1917 when the pain from the rheumatism became so bad that he checked in to St. Joseph's Infirmary in Hot Springs, Arkansas, for treatment, he began to accept the Maryknoll work within his spiritual context.[15] He finally wrote on March 25, 1918 concerning his experience during prayer:

> You seemed certainly to grant the prayers and you seemed to tell us over again that you were the Immaculate Conception and that we need fear nothing that our work would certainly succeed fully because it was yours, and this seemed to mean that we should (continue) our work within the Society (Maryknoll) and then the completion outside in the general work for needs that can't be otherwise supplied etc., . . .

This is also expressed in the editor's notes in *The Lily of Mary: Bernadette of Lourdes* with its dedication to foreign missions.[16]

By 1918 we see a man who found unity in his ongoing spiritual relationships and acceptance of his work. For Fred the final gift of unity was to come after James Anthony's return to Maryknoll after scouting the Far East for a Maryknoll mission territory.

China Mission (1918–1919)

Fred was overjoyed with the news that he would lead the first mission band to China. He was looking forward to spreading the Church's teachings along with the prospect of martyrdom at the hands of the Chinese.

"Before leaving for China in 1918, Price made certain that the Carmelite Sisters in Baltimore had both his mission and himself in their prayers."[17] The relationship was an extremely deep one between Fred and the Carmel. The letters of Fred to Sr. Regina Holmes, O.C.D., in 1917–1918 reveal their "pact of martyrdom," which was a spiritual bond between a missionary priest and a contemplative sister.[18]

In September 1918, the first Maryknoll mission band left for China with Fred as the leader. Fathers James Edward Walsh, Francis X. Ford, and Bernard Meyer were the young Maryknollers in the band. Once at the mission location in Yeungkong, China, which was named Lourdes, the Maryknollers began learning Chinese in earnest. Fred's tremendous difficulty with this language and increased suffering from rheumatism are perhaps put in perspective by this description from the *Tarheel Apostle:*

He had never learned to say more in their language than the simple greetings, "How are you?" and "God bless you!" Even those two brief expressions were learned only by constant repetition and perhaps at times the enunciation of them could not pass muster with the critical. But his children in Christ had realized what he meant to say, the love that he wanted thereby to show them, and they had been intensely attracted to him. Somehow they found something not only unusual, but also inspiring, in the sight of this elderly priest, stammering their language, crippled by their climate, yet smiling and serene, and ever forgetful of self and mindful of them. . . . With their gift for finding suitable names, they simply referred to the veteran missioner as "the holy priest,". . . .[19]

Death

Though Father Bernadette was very ill with rheumatism in China's damp climate, it was an aching tooth that convinced him to seek medical help in Hong Kong. After making the painful journey to Hong Kong, he also developed appendicitis. The chains he put on in August 1911, he was still wearing. He supposedly told the nurse who discovered the chains that he had without regret lost the key to them years before. The severe infection from the appendicitis led to several days of suffering and then to his death on September 12, 1919, the feast of the Holy Name of Mary.[20]

Fred's life was one of proclaiming the Church's teaching based on a personal relationship with the Blessed Mother who healed and guided the Tarheel in his mission and to his beloved Bernadette Soubirous. His spiritual marriage with Bernadette was a great joy to Fred. He struggled many years trying to be a saint and realized the shortcomings of his own life, especially his pride. Fred experienced much pain in his life—physical pain from the rheumatism and the purgation of sleeping on the floor and psychological pain with the betrayal at Nazareth and the losses of Nazareth and *Truth* with the beginning of Maryknoll. Lastly, there was the pain in the rejection of key parts of his mission vision.

Notes

1. *Diary,* 536.
2. *Diary,* 537.
3. John C. Murrett, *Tarheel,* 147.
4. *Diary,* 578, 597, 611.
5. *Diary,* 534.
6. *Diary,* 614–5.
7. *Diary,* 766–9.
8. Raymond A. Lane, *The Early Days of Maryknoll* (New York: McKay, 1951) 124–6.
9. John C. Murrett, *Tarheel,* 153.
10. Thomas Frederick Price, ed., *Bernadette of Lourdes* (New York: Devin-Adair, 1914).
11. Thomas Frederick Price, ed., *The Lily of Mary: Bernadette of Lourdes* (New York: Bureau of the Immaculate Conception, 1918).
12. Thomas Frederick Price, *Collected Letters,* 109.
13. Thomas Frederick Price, *Collected Letters,* 110–1.
14. *Diary,* 2653–70; for a discussion of the tension between the founders, see Robert E. Sheridan, *The Founders of Maryknoll* (Maryknoll: The Catholic Foreign Mission Society of America, Inc., 1980) 79–97.
15. *Diary,* 2902.
16. Thomas Frederick Price, ed., *The Lily of Mary,* 20.
17. Colette Ackerman and Joseph Healey, "Bonded in Mission: Reflections on Prayer and Evangelization" (unpublished manuscript) 5.
18. Ackerman and Healey, "Bonded," 12.
19. John C. Murrett, *Tarheel,* 225. For an earlier version of this account, see George C. Powers Biography of Fr. Thomas Frederick Price (untitled, unpublished manuscript, Maryknoll Society Archives, 1943) 216. For the original version, see Patrick J. Byrne, *Father Price of Maryknoll,* (Maryknoll, N.Y.: Catholic Foreign Mission Society, 1923) 53–6.
20. John C. Murrett, *Tarheel,* 233–8.

10

Journey to Marriage
and Beyond*

The "introduction" of Fred to Bernadette, as we have seen, occurred during his first visit to Lourdes in July 1911. The friendship developed into a deep relationship as Fred experienced the presence of Bernadette. He began a spiritual journey of ever-increasing union with Bernadette that led to a deeper relationship with the Blessed Mother, Jesus, and the Trinity. These unions were marked by marriage ceremonies, consecrations, and renewal of vows.

The relationship between Fred and Bernadette followed the basic pattern of a man and woman in love: introduction, courtship, betrothal/marriage, and deepening union, which emerged in what he called an "annihilation in Bernadette." To him "annihilation" meant loss of self-centeredness, an awareness of self in the moments of total self-giving to and receiving of the beloved. He was not talking about his physical being but rather about his spiritual self. At the center of this union was Jesus. This led to a second marriage of the united spouses (Bernadette and Fred) to Jesus, their divine Spouse. In this union the couple experiences annihilation in the Holy Trinity.

*This chapter analyzes the experiential developments in Fred's life after his visit to Lourdes in July 1911. The events between July 1911 and September 1919 were shaped by the "miracle," as Fred called it, that happened during that first visit to Lourdes.

Blocks to the Relationship

We saw how Fred was initially affected by his first visit to Lourdes and how the events in Dublin had reoriented his spiritual and emotional life away from the Ignatian Exercises and towards not a program but a person, Bernadette. This change should not be minimized in any way. What Fred experienced at Lourdes during that first visit was for him a "Copernican revolution," opening new vistas of his spiritual understanding and turning his method of prayer in another direction: "I learned more in a few hours at Lourdes than I learned in my life and I felt there as never before the utter powerlessness of all human means and methods in the spiritual life which have not efficacy of themselves but only through the spirit of God."[1]

The Ignatian Exercises were immediately seen as a great hindrance to his new spiritual life:

> Under this influence it seemed to me that the plans concerning Ignatian methods were hindering me and should be dropped and the 30 day retreat began to appear also a hindrance. . . . I should make only a short retreat . . . and go back to Lourdes . . . . P and H giving myself solely to Jesus and you praying and doing penance for sinners . . . My heart burns and burns for you over and over and I am trying to get back to Lourdes which seems my only real Home on earth because you were there. . . . My Mother, at Lourdes you have changed my whole life.[2]

However, it was not until May 1915 when "Bernadette" writes in the *Diary* that the exercises were no longer a part of his life:

> St. Ignatius' exercises . . . seemed totally out of his spirit now when he looked at them to-day and he felt he could not use them. I have changed him from them completely to me in obedience to your command at the grotto when you told my poor spouse to drop the Exercises of St. Ignatius as not suited for him and to take *me*.[3]

During the trip to Dublin in July 1911 Bernadette became the focal point of his return to Lourdes, and again in Lourdes it was clear to Fred that his mission was Bernadette.

There were some blocks to Fred's attempt to do Bernadette's work or mission. Over the remaining years he discovered that he had tremendous pride in his plans to "do that" and great ambition to "achieve this." Eventually he saw this pride as self-reliance and ambition as self-confidence and English paganism.[4] With this new dedication to Bernadette, this planning (which he never really gave up) became irrelevant to his real mission of being one with Bernadette. Thus, the Mission Center at Nazareth, North Carolina had to go for it was a symbol of *his* achievement and *his* plans. Furthermore gaining spiritual self-control through the Ignatian Exercises filled him with pride;[5] they were a block to his life with Bernadette. They too had to go.

The Growing Relationship

On July 10, 1911, he summarized his first visit to Lourdes:

> The Blessed Virgin in a moment of the most exquisite sweetness seemed to me [to] grant three things and any planned prayer disappeared. These were that I would always be like her and Jesus, that as Jesus lived in her He would live in me but of course with infinitude of difference. In the lowest way she in the highest— Also that the Nazareth would be a production of Him in the same way and also the foundation of Foreign Mission, the same but differently. . . . what my Mother wanted was simplicity and purity and humility and she seemed to turn away from me and would not answer my prayers for Nazareth. I have seldom felt so troubled. . . . I have feared that my making the Exercises and merely my whole life was a huge act of pride and passion. Moreover the simple life of Bernadette has greatly impressed me.[6]

This he states over and over again until his death in 1919. It is the theme that echoes through the *Diary:* "to be like Bernadette," "to be one with Bernadette," "to be Bernadette." She was Fred's model for living: "If I pass my life as Bernadette with her purity, humility, and detachment, doing simply with all my heart whatever work God marked out for me, I would count my life the highest success."[7]

Even though pride and ambition blurred his mission "to be Bernadette," the objective to be a saint, "to have Jesus living in him," was fulfilled. His dedication to Bernadette, the Blessed Mother and Jesus, combined with his problems at Nazareth and at Maryknoll, made them his only friends.[8] The struggle for new paths of humility, simplicity, and poverty provided the purgations he would pursue. Seeking humiliations and accepting them became his desire. Humiliations included failure to solicit funds from parishes he approached, Father Walsh's admonitions, and criticism by others. Fred's scrupulosity was a recurring problem also, whether it was over the use of funds, dealing with people, or adhering to the rubrics when celebrating Mass.[9]

Temptations and Jealousy

At the same time Fred's love for and attraction to Bernadette was increasing, secular fashions were becoming more and more revealing. Plunging necklines and exposed skin became the cultural norm. As his love for and attraction to Bernadette increased, immodest dress in women bothered him. He mentioned it over and over again in the *Diary*.[10]

He feared being seduced away from Bernadette and was "tortured being in the company of young women" dressed in the new revealing fashions: "Also, Mother, it has grown to me to be a torture to be thrown into the company of young women especially where they adopt the custom of <not> having their bodies any way uncovered as is the custom with many nowadays."[11]

At one point the *Diary* reported that interior trials were threatening Fred's life with Bernadette.[12] When James Walsh allowed women to attend services in the chapel, Fred lodged a strong but unsuccessful protest.[13] He made significant efforts to avoid women. He would not wear his prescription glasses, but rather, wore sunglasses so that his nearsightedness and the darkness would make it difficult to see:[14]

> Mother, I spoke to the Academy of the Sacred Heart in Hoboken. I did not like to refuse when asked but I thought it likely I would meet with much immodest dressing there and I did. I put on dark glasses when speaking but [the] immodest dressing of those girls was vile—I felt to some extent like vomiting. I do not think I can bring myself to speak again to young women on account of this immodest dressing unless forced and then I shall wear the darkest glasses that I may not see them. It seems to me, Mother, all sense

of modesty is gone for these women—good Catholic women—though I know them to be innocent as children. Help me, my sweet Bride, to be true to you for ever.[15]

Once he asked to sleep on a train to avoid the immodest women.[16] He would place Lourdes water on his eyes as well.[17]

Temptations of the flesh were at times great and torturous;[18] at times he used severe mortifications (self-flagellation).[19] The chains that Fred wore were not for mortification; rather they were a sign of slavery and consecration. One chain was for his slavery to the Blessed Mother, another for his slavery to Bernadette, and a third for Bernadette and Fred together being consecrated to the Blessed Mother.[20]

Fred's almost constant fear of being seduced away from Bernadette was spiritual as well as physical. Included in this problem were his reading about or following the life of Teresa of Avila and relationships with the sisters in the Baltimore Carmel.[21]

Focusing on Bernadette and remaining faithful to her was most important: "The following . . . . came to me, Mother, to-day—to cut out the attraction to the Carmelite Sisters and certain saints that may interfere with my attraction to Lourdes, for they seem temptations of the devil."[22] Therefore, he initially rejected the idea of a Baltimore Carmelite nun having him as a spiritual brother: "The idea of one of the Carmelites having me for a spiritual brother seemed to me to interfere with Sister's life and right over my heart, I have rejected it."[23]

His spiritual guardedness was not just with regard to women. While at Saint Anne de Beaupré in Quebec on a retreat, Fred ran into his old friend Father Irwin from North Carolina, who recommended that Fred visit Brother André at the Holy Cross College in Montreal for his healing prayer. Fred rejected his friend's urging because it would be a spiritual distraction.[24]

Courtship and Betrothal

Fred's experience of Bernadette was constantly increasing. It grew from a special presence during the all-night vigil at her tomb in the convent at Nevers to feeling her presence in him constantly.[25]

He was concerned over these new experiences in his life and consulted with two spiritual directors, Fr. Pierre Paul Chapon, S.S., of St. Mary's Seminary, and a Father O'Rourke, S.J., who lived in New York.[26] They both read key parts of the *Diary* and gave their approval to Fred's relationship with Bernadette and the spiritual marriages.

Chapon, after reading the *Diary* notebooks that dealt with the 1911 visit to Lourdes, suggested that Bernadette was Fred's "lady of the castle" and that he was her "knight."[27] Later the union deepened into a more intimate relationship than a knight admiring his lady from afar. This was not a problem for Fred, who understood the chivalry of Southern culture, the lady of the castle was to be one's wife. Chapon gave Fred Fr. M. J. Ribet's *La Mystique Divine* to read.[28] He hoped that the mystical marriage described in the book would parallel Fred's experience.[29]

By January 1912 Fred writes: "In other words, Mother, Sister and I will live totally for you and you will make us totally Jesus."[30] In that month Father Bernadette changed the signature on the daily letter in the *Diary* from "Mary Bernadette N.[azareth] of Jesus" to just "Mary Bernadette."[31] The summer of 1912 saw Fred consecrate himself to Bernadette, which was approved by Father Chapon. After that time the sense that his relationship with Bernadette was that of a marriage increased. The betrothal period was filled with the joy of Bernadette's presence and the pain of her absence. He asked that the Blessed Mother arrange that Bernadette and Fred be one soul.[32] On March 24 Fred writes:

> My heart is filled with delight, Mother, and to-night Sister came to me in the fullest possession of me and stayed with me for a long time—as my Bride and my Spouse forever and poured out herself upon me in unspeakable delights. Truly, Mother, you have married us—our souls—and our bodies in a way—and we are one—and spouses—and she my eternal Bride. Oh Mother, it seems to me the most wonderful and greatest grace imaginable—for you to give me Sister—as my Bride my Spouse for ever—and if you would give me [to choose] of all things of Jesus's creation except you I would choose this.[33]

Several days later he wrote:

A thought which seemed to me surely of God because it brings such light and peace and happiness is that I should pray constantly and that I should never doubt that B[ernadette] and I are one—body and soul—for all eternity—that she alone should be and I should be her slave for all eternity and to carry out her sweet will for all eternity and that for all eternity I should never love anything except her and her sweet will and that she should make me one victim with her and you and Jesus.[34]

Bernadette urged Fred to ask the Blessed Mother that they be granted "complete and full union with her as contained in our marriage."[35] He asked for union body and soul.

En route to becoming one being, body and soul with Bernadette, Fred describes moments as ecstasy, almost ecstasy, unspeakable delights, Bernadette absorbing him, being overpowered by her, drowned out by her possession, and of being transported out of himself. She gave him "unspeakable gifts," caused the utmost happiness, and came with great favors and overpowering sweetness. He is wounded with sweet love. His heart bleeds over her.[36] It is obvious that their relationship, even in the early stages, was moving rapidly beyond the lady in the castle and her knight.

To Fred, Bernadette was the purest and sweetest name except Jesus. She was his supreme mistress, and he was deeply in love with her body and soul. She became his only vocation, his mission, and he wanted to be an extension of her, having no other care. He was her slave as they were the Blessed Mother's. Fred believed that the Blessed Mother give him the name "Marie Bernadette" in September 1912. He immediately started to use his new name in the *Diary,* and a year later he began using the name or initials "M. B." in public. He felt that it was his duty to follow Bernadette and, in keeping with his usual practice, sought and received Pierre Chapon's approval to follow her. Father Bernadette was so dedicated to her that he would not eat apples for they reminded her of the fall in Eden, but he would eat grapes for they reminded Bernadette of the Eucharist.[37]

As part of his plans to carry out Bernadette's mission, he worked to have Estrades' *Life of Bernadette* translated and published and to found a mission society. The Bureau of the Immaculate Conception was founded and two editions of the book were published, but the mission society, dedicated to the mission activity in the United States and the Philippines, did not materialize.[38]

The honeymoon itself was a time of deepening presence and joy. His attempts to give descriptions of the possession are never complete and are really only hints. Once he wrote:

> I have been greatly puzzled, Mother, in reading Ribet's *Mystique Divine.* I cannot find anything like my case there and my union—marriage—as I called it with Sister's soul is an altogether different thing from what is spoken there in the matter of union. Mine is an intense desire of union to be one with Sister—so that we [may] be as it were one slave before you and one spouse of Jesus.[39]

Chapon had helped relieve Fred's fear of losing Bernadette's presence and any separation from her by assuring him that Bernadette is always present to him whether or not he notices it.[40]

The Wedding

By the spring of 1913, Bernadette tells Fred to purchase a wedding ring. He does so immediately and has the silver wedding band engraved with "M. B. + M. B." The cross represents Jesus as the link between them. Formal wedding vows were "said" according to church rites.[41] Initially Fred kept the ring on a chain around his neck since priests did not wear such rings; for brief moments he would wear it on his finger. That experience gave him such joy that he covered it with a leather band and wore it on the ring finger of his left hand.[42] Later he petitioned Rome, with the help of Cardinal Gibbons, so that he might wear it (his request was eventually denied, but the reply arrived after his death).

From the ceremony on there was a strong sense of being wed and that the marriage would be "consummated" at Lourdes and Nevers during his summer pilgrimage in 1913. While in France he said the following vow at the Lourdes grotto and at her tomb in Nevers: "With this ring I, M[arie] B[ernadette] wed thee M[arie] B[ernadette] body and soul for all eternity so that you are absorbed body and soul into my being for all eternity and for all eternity we form one being in which I alone am; and I plight unto thee my troth for ever. R.[Response] Amen. Amen. My own beloved all."[43] He celebrated the wedding by having a cigar and some wine as Bernadette directed, the first smoke he ever had and the first wine he ever drank outside of the Eucharist. Along with his joy, he has concerns, however, over the relationship with Bernadette being a hindrance to communication with the Blessed Mother, Jesus, and the Trinity.[44] After returning to the United States, Fred reports being one with Bernadette and annihilated in her:

> Finally during the Exposition of the Blessed Sacrament there (Lourdes Grotto in Brooklyn) at Benediction—as if you, Mother, and my Bride sent me to our Lord for [a] cure—the light and peace came. It came to me clear and true—that I am and was to be—one being with my Bride and lost in her body and soul—in this way: By her physical possession of my body and soul are lost physically in her so it seems to me and so it seems to me that it will be for ever—and that still more lost in her spiritually in the fact that our Lord gives me to love her so much that whatever she loves I love with all my heart. . . . That is we are so one that we love Jesus with one heart—Bernadette's heart and so we feel and act one being—one heart—to God.[45]

Reflections

During sessions with his spiritual directors, the discussion of whether or not others had experienced what Fred was going through must have been talked about. He writes that the assigned readings his spiritual advisor had given him were not exactly like his own experience. Fortunately, a few months later he checked the *Catholic Encyclopedia* concerning "Contemplation":

> It seemed to me that characteristics given to contempl[ation] applied to me and my Bride's life; and that the mystic marriage between my Bride and me was largely as put there—her presence and possession of me and the oneness of life and my annihilation in her. I doubt after reading whether I ever had an intellectual vision—I am not sure. In fact I can find nothing anywhere that fits exactly my Bride's case and mine, and it seems to me that my duty is if I understand Father Chapon to follow the attractions you and my Bride give me, and according to these we are one being, body and soul—forever I her slave and spouse annihilated in her for ever and she as it were alone existing and I absorbed in her living

her life knowing nothing but her and doing her will for ever—this of course with due subordination—i.e. to you and Jesus whom we love infinitely more than ourselves—I live now not I but she lives in me for ever; we live now not we but Jesus lives in us for ever; it seems to me that nothing else would ever satisfy my heart. . . .[46]

The next day, November 23, 1913, he writes concerning his spiritual marriage to Bernadette after reading the articles in the *Catholic Encyclopedia* on "Mystic Marriage" and "Spiritual Marriage:"

When the mystics say that they live in God's life and think by His thought, and love by His love and will by His will—they believe according to appearances and what they feel and so it seems, though this is not entirely true but there are facets which seem to be thus . . . that we are one being that I live by her life, that I think by her thoughts, love by her love, and will by her will, and there seems to be only one being in me thinking and loving and willing and that being not I but my sweet Bride and my happiness is unspeakable. I cannot explain how it is so, but so it seems, with a consciousness and knowledge which I cannot explain and it would seem to tear my being asunder if it should not be so for ever. I feel that this is why you gave me my sweet Bride's name long before you formally married us—that you intend me to be annihilated in her and that she alone would live in me, and so you named me truly, Marie Bernadette, for she alone—not I,—lives in me.[47]

To Fred the relationship between Bernadette and himself was

a peculiar one—not to be found in books etc., not exactly mystic marriage in the strict technical sense yet in the wide sense—one in which my Bride and I are one being as it were—that I live, as it were, her life—and will and love and think as it were her will and love and thoughts—That this is the attraction and whilst it is different from any other that I know of—that I am to follow it up as far as I can because it is your attraction and what you wish of me, it seems to me, Mother, that this continuous sentiment in me is the basis—in me day and night—is the effect of my Bride's being in me having possession of me being one with me—that this sentiment may be the same but weak except when I am in prayer that then it becomes strong but is the same, running into higher contemplation and at times the lighter stages of ecstasy—and this seems to be borne out by what the *C[atholic] Encyclopedia* says namely, that the presence—*borders on* the constitutive essential element of the mystic marriage in the strict sense. At any rate my duty is clear—to leave books and explanations alone—and follow what you indicate—and that is that I should be annihilated in my Bride, and my Bride alone should be in me, I living her life and breathing it and thinking her thoughts and with her love and will alone as it were in me. . . .[48]

In summary, the characteristics of "Mystical Union" described in the *Catholic Encyclopedia*[49] are

1. A feeling of the presence
2. An interior possession (in making presence felt)
3. The mystical union cannot be produced at will.
4. Knowledge of God is obscured and confused.
5. Communication is only half comprehensible.
6. Contemplation of God is not by reasoning or by external or internal images.
7. There are continual fluctuations in intensity of the union.
8. It does not involve intensive labor on the part of the recipient.
9. It is accompanied by an impulse towards virtue.
10. There is a state of quiet and interior acts are curtailed.
11. The body is acted upon.

In addition to these characteristics, the semi-ecstatic or full ecstatic state is described as entire union and the spiritual marriage state as transforming union. The difference in these states is a matter of intensity. This would explain the changing qualifiers that Fred uses in the *Diary* such as "delights," "ecstasy," and "presence."

Along with the above characteristics of spirituality, the *Catholic Encyclopedia* discusses mystical marriage, such as those between female saints and Christ. For male saints, such as John of the Cross, it was between Christ and the saint's soul (the spiritual nature of the inner man).[50] Using St. Teresa of Avila's model, the transforming union has three elements: continual sense of presence, a consciousness of participating on a supernatural level, and "an habitual intellectual vision of the Blessed Trinity or of some Divine attribute."[51]

On to Mystical Union

As the journey on the unitive way continued, Bernadette and Fred experienced an increasing presence of Jesus as their divine Spouse. The experiences Fred had of Bernadette and they of Jesus ranged from happiness, to presence, to delights, to sweetness, to possession, to union and ecstasy. The experiences should be thought of as running along a spectrum rather than isolated events. Within each category listed above there are variations. Happiness was described as exquisite, infinite, intoxicating, ineffable, inexpressible. "Delights" and "sweetness" often appeared in conjunction with the other experiences. The delights were expressed as inconceivable or unspeakable; "heavenly" and "eternal" were used to describe events of union and possession. At times he stated that exquisite spiritual events overpowered him day and night in his relationship with Bernadette, Jesus, and the Holy Trinity. At times during periods of possession, it was as if only Bernadette existed. She was enthroned in his heart.[52]

Bernadette took possession so fully that Fred believed that she was writing the letters to the Blessed Mother for both of them. On February 11, 1915, the day after they consecrated themselves to the Blessed Mother and put another chain on Father Bernadette, the letters are addressed "Our own loved Mother" instead of "My own loved Mother and Bride." They are signed "Marie Bernadette and Marie Bernadette."[53] The letters from this time on are as if written by Bernadette and express not so much her inner thoughts and feelings as they report to the Blessed Mother concerning her "poor spouse's" activities, thoughts, and feelings. Bernadette writes in the *Diary* that

> to-day my poor spouse seemed to understand that in our inter-
> course we are one in body and soul; he annihilated in me and I
> possessing him body and soul, and in this he continually gives his
> whole being to me but that at times I take him entirely to myself
> so that in me he is conscious only of me and absorbed in me in a
> sort of ecstasy and this seemed to take place to-day when I alone
> seemed to exist in him and brought delights inconceivable.[54]

As the union between Fred and Bernadette has them at the point of becoming "one being" and Fred overwhelmed in

Bernadette, it should be noted that early in their relationship Jesus emerges at the center of their marriage. Fred writes in November 1912:

> I believe to be true and in a sense know to be true—that Sister and I live between ourselves and with you [the Blessed Mother] the very same life—the life of Jesus who communicates His adorable life to us by grace so that we are one really and truly living the same divine life which is common to us and by this we are one and be it Sister and I and you in a sense are one being and by it I live my life with Sister which you have given me and am her slave and carry out the wishes of her sweet heart.[55]

This develops into a love relationship between Fred and Bernadette as one being and the bride of Jesus their divine spouse. The presence of Jesus becomes an ever-growing experience in the midst of their own union. However, just as the marriage between Bernadette and Fred developed over time, so did the experience of the divine Presence.

Marriage to Jesus

In early 1915 the spiritual experiences took a deepening turn. While in a state of ecstasy in Bernadette, Fred was presented by her to the Blessed Mother and the Holy Trinity. A rapidly increasing presence of Jesus for Bernadette and Fred had been building since their marriage in 1913. In July 1914 Fred believes that Jesus has then given his name as well. Now Fred is "Jesus Marie Bernadette." On March 3, 1915, a novena is begun in preparation for the initial nuptials which were to be the beginning of eternal life as one being with Jesus in Heaven. A "special union" with Jesus as one with them was felt on Easter. The marriage took place on April 7, 1915, with the saying of vows at Holy Communion and saying them again and singing the *Magnificat* at their secret shrine in the woods. Bernadette and Fred experienced a deeper union with each other, Jesus and the Holy Spirit. On April 15, they reported having the "most exquisite delights" uniting them to Jesus and the Holy Trinity.[56]

The wedding ring portrayed the spiritual situation. Bernadette gave Fred "the idea of having my name and his in my lily—the words to be "IHS" that is 'to M. B. M. B.' placed inside the lily for I am the Lily, Mother. . . ."[57] A cross was placed in the center of the lily.[58]

Bernadette continued to give herself to Fred, stating that "I should give [him] my PURITY, HUMILITY—MY DETACHMENT, LOVE OF YOU AND JESUS AND THE CROSS—my love for sinners—that it is his want of these things that keep[s] him from being me."[59] At times their union with each other ends in them resting in the divine Majesty. The *Diary* records this greater union with Jesus:

> Today we received a more intimate communication and union with our Divine Spouse than ever before, Mother. "We seemed to be one in Jesus and the Holy Trinity—lost in them in the ineffable effusions of Divine love and this lasted for a long time—upwards of half an hour or so."[60] The relationship between the couple and Jesus deepened rapidly: "We seemed to rest largely in Jesus—together—his spouse and slave annihilated in Him— amidst inconceivable delights . . . every day we feel more and more annihilated in our Divine Spouse.[61]

Also during this time the couple together experienced being transported out of themselves into the Trinity or being one with Jesus. A few months later, as the relationship continued to deepen, on July 4, 1916, Bernadette writes "that we are one body and soul in the Divine Majesty who is in us and through us producing us and making us one being, annihilated in the Holy Trinity and this thought is so powerful and so sweet that we are thrown almost into ecstasy by it."[62]

On February 25, 1917, the marriage with Jesus *Hostia* (Jesus Suffering) was effected. It was Jesus *Hostia* who possessed them.[63] This union with the suffering Jesus and his presence during the Stations of the Cross and at Mass with Fred and Bernadette can be understood by working through the concept of the cross that runs through the *Diary*. The wedding symbol, i.e., the lily on the ring, is one of the keys to understanding this situation.

The Cross

The cross in the center of the lily on the ring graphically represents Fred's life in Bernadette and Jesus together with his day-to-day living. Earlier in the *Diary* the Catholic Foreign Mission

Society (Maryknoll) was seen by Fred as his cross.[64] Then the humiliations he experienced were seen as purgations and a means of perfection for him. Bernadette is seen as the purgation/cross giver. At the same time, however, the suffering unites the couple. In this context Bernadette sees herself as the structure of the cross

FIGURE #2

THE RING: MARRIAGE INSCRIPTION
Symbolizing the Marriage of the Couple to Jesus[65]

in the lily.[66] Later the Blessed Mother wants Bernadette to annihilate (via their union) Fred on the cross with Jesus:

> You wanted me to nail my poor spouse to the cross and he should hang there all his life—I in him—with me and you and Jesus—on the cross (and that he should have nothing but me and we one being hanging on the cross) and this idea fastened on his soul and seemed to be of you and my poor spouse embraced it fully in as much as it was from you.[67]

The cross is also martyrdom, and Fred does pray for actual martyrdom. Marriage itself is eventually seen as crucifixion for the spouse, a self giving: "We are to turn to Him—our spouse—the victim on the Cross and [we] thank Him for making us one victim with Him and you."[68] It is worth noting also that, Fred is a victim via the pain of crippling rheumatism. As a victim he is poured out to Jesus.[69]

In the marriage to Jesus there was also an experience of martyrdom. The link to martyrdom was their martyred bodies being given up to the beloved.[70] As mentioned above, the lily on the ring with the two M. B.s shows the unity in crucifixion. Towards the end of his life, Fred seems to reject actual martyrdom in favor of the martyrdom of self-giving to another. He sees a conflict between praying for actual martyrdom as contradictory to giving of oneself in long-term mission service.[71] For Fred mission remained the glory of their divine Spouse, the glory of God. Finally, in September 1919, the *Diary* expresses the mission completed as Bernadette writes

> I made him feel that through me—with me—he is made into Jesus—we are one being in Jesus—and that you and Jesus have made me after you his all—his life—his sweetness—his hope that by being me he possesses Jesus and we are together one child of yours, and I give him a foretaste of our life in heaven.[72]

This completes Fred Price's objective as stated in the initial Lourdes experience, i.e., to be a saint, to live in Jesus.

Lourdes: a Conversion Experience

At the core of this feeling of union between Bernadette and Fred, and his original spiritual objective, is the experience of Jesus. As they become one, the *Diary* expresses that they are one slave to the Blessed Mother and that she has given them the gift of spiritual marriage. They are as one united with Jesus, their Spouse, in a second spiritual marriage in the spring of 1915. The next several years involve a deepening union with Jesus and annihilation in the Holy Trinity. A special union with the Blessed Mother occurred in July 1917. Unfortunately, it is the only section of the *Diary* that is missing. Another consecration took place in 1919. It was of both Fred and Bernadette to St. Joseph as their spiritual father.[73]

The Lourdes event combines the experience of a mystic/ spiritual marriage with Marian spirituality for Fred. This creates a unity of the two independent paths that affected him. There are no indications that he was aware of the spiritual marriage possibilities upon his first visit to Lourdes. These developments, however, were based more on personal experience in prayer than theological or devotional training.

As seen during the discussion of the Rebecca Clyde sinking, deep mystical conversion experiences have with them a sense of liberation, awareness of the nearness of God, an outpouring of love for God, and an other-than-self world view.[74] The liberation that is given to Fred is that of being released from the Nazareth ministry. The nearness felt is that of Bernadette and the Blessed Mother, not of God directly. The love experienced by Fred is that of Bernadette's for him and through that Jesus' presence. Finally, he develops an other-than-self view, the mission to be carried out by Fred is not his but Bernadette's. This is a tremendous change for him.

Fred's Heart

In 1919 after his death from appendicitis, Father Bernadette was buried in Hong Kong. His heart, where he felt the indwelling of his Lady, was brought to Nevers, France. As he had wished it was placed in the convent chapel crypt beside the body of Bernadette. In 1936, when Fr. James Anthony Walsh died, Father Price's body was returned to Maryknoll, New York, and placed in the cemetery with the other co-founder. Later, with the building of a new chapel, their bodies were placed beside each other in the crypt directly under the high altar. Fred's body might still be with Maryknoll, but his heart belonged to his beloved Bernadette.

Notes

1. *Diary,* 540.
2. *Diary,* 537.
3. *Diary,* 2204.
4. *Diary,* 977, 1258.
5. *Diary,* 537.
6. *Diary,* 534.
7. *Diary,* 569.
8. *Diary,* 1188.
9. *Diary,* 1285.
10. *Diary,* 674, 894, 901, 902–A, 903, 913, 916, 938, 1125, 1297, 1302–4, 1329, 1330, 1342, 1352, 1379, 1383, 1384, 1406–8, 1420, 1478, 1482–5, 1502, 1508, 1516, 1535, 1537–40, 1549, 1557, 1560, 1565, 1566, 1572, 1559, 1660, 1664, 1669, 1676, 1681, 1682, 1709, 1731, 1732, 1744, 1760, 1761, 1769, 1776, 1782, 1833, 1844–6, 1851, 1853–5, 1862, 1875, 1879, 1880, 1887, 1904, 1919, 1937, 1953, 1955, 1983, 1992, 2002, 2010, 2072, 2082, 2177, 2184, 2218, 2226, 2243, 2247, 2248, 2262, 2276, 2278, 2279, 2294, 2311, 2312, 2339, 2460, 2566, 2577, 2621, 2636, 2659, 2675, 2746, 2753, 2796, 2803, 2815, 2843, 2891, 2909, 3053, 3117, 3175, 3199, 3225, 3235, 3557.

11. *Diary,* 894.
12. *Diary,* 1898.
13. *Diary,* 1089–90.
14. *Diary,* 1478, 1664, 1390.
15. *Diary,* 1663.
16. *Diary,* 1776.
17. *Diary,* 1344.
18. *Diary,* 625, 1010, 1324, 1328, 1342, 1358, 1424, 1577, 1629–31, 1679, 1683, 1685, 1782, 2064.
19. *Diary,* 2259.
20. *Diary,* 2087.
21. *Diary,* 1560, 3177.
22. *Diary,* 791.
23. *Diary,* 919.
24. *Diary,* 1896.
25. *Diary,* 1282, 1284, 1285.
26. Chapon's spiritual direction was in the traditional Sulpician style (Christopher J. Kauffman, *Tradition and Transformation in Catholic Culture* [New York: Macmillan, 1988]) and O'Rourke gave the Jesuit perspective. *Diary,* 945.
27. *Diary,* 1039.
28. M. J. Ribet, *La Mystique Divine* (Paris: Libairie Ch. Poussielque, 1895); *Diary,* 1124.
29. *Diary,* 1039, 1124, 1137, 1140, 1202.
30. *Diary,* 755.
31. *Diary,* 766-769.
32. *Diary,* 1093.
33. *Diary,* 1289.
34. *Diary,* 1301. He compiled (*Diary* 1301, 1323; see also 1093, 1284).
35. *Diary,* 1323.
36. *Diary,* 1100, 1107, 1116, 1117, 1133, 1138–9, 1152, 1192, 1201, 1219–20, 1228, 1240, 1272, 1284, 1296, 1314.
37. *Diary,* 1097, 1104, 1175, 1187, 1188, 1200, 1234, 1235, 1243, 1247, 1258, 1266, 1301, 1331, 1335.
38. *Diary,* 1295, 1312, 1313.
39. *Diary,* 1140.
40. *Diary,* 1172, 1204, 1208, 1285.
41. *Diary,* 1036-7.
42. *Diary,* 1308, 1309, 1314, 1316.
43. *Diary,* 1422.
44. *Diary,* 1454.

45. *Diary,* 1475–6.
46. *Diary,* 1593.
47. *Diary,* 1594–5.
48. *Diary,* 1603–04.
49. *Catholic Encyclopedia,* (New York: The Encyclopedia Press, 1910) "Contemplation" by Poulain.
50. *Catholic Encyclopedia,* "Soul" by Michael Maher and Joseph Boland.
51. *Catholic Encyclopedia,* "Marriage, Mystical" by Poulain.
52. *Diary,* 1156, 1225, 1228, 1289, 1294, 1302, 1321, 1325, 1331, 1340, 1342, 1348, 1370, 1377, 1382, 1386, 1387, 1438, 1460, 1471, 1477, 1487, 1508, 1515, 1528, 1565, 1570, 1583, 1588, 1608, 1615, 1626, 1652, 1669–70, 1673, 1711, 1721, 1727–8, 1741, 1749, 1787, 1791, 1818, 1840, 1843, 1847, 1854, 1877, 1893, 1898, 1918, 1920, 1930, 1933–4, 1941, 1952, 1959, 1960, 1966, 1981, 2005, 2008, 2017, 2028, 2042, 2061–2, 2072–3, 2094, 2145, 2151, 2159, 2164, 2175, 2178–80, 2184, 2194, 2233, 2236–7, 2241, 2245, 2254, 2611, 2261, 2264, 2277, 2281, 2418, 2422, 2429, 2454, 2458, 2469, 2493, 2534, 2574, 2577, 2588, 2611, 2662, 2713, 2743, 2746, 2964, 2989, 3137, 3141, 3147, 3486, 3970.
53. *Diary,* 2087–9.
54. *Diary,* 2544.
55. *Diary,* 1143, 1358, 1374, 1729, 1920, 2068.
56. *Diary,* 2107, 2144, 2148, 2153, 2155, 2157–65.
57. *Diary,* 2144.
58. Robert E. Sheridan, ed., *A Symposium,* 182.
59. *Diary,* 2188.
60. *Diary,* 2199, 2567.
61. *Diary,* 2574.
62. *Diary,* 2613. See also 2430, 2459, 2577, 2586.
63. *Diary,* 2865.
64. *Diary,* 1793, 1834.
65. Robert E. Sheridan, ed., *The Symposium,* 181–2.
66. *Diary,* 1972, 1999, 2015.
67. *Diary,* 2316.
68. *Diary,* 2738, 3134, 3147, 3286.
69. *Diary,* 3168–9, 3277, 3289.
70. *Diary,* 3141, 4144, 4145, 3148, 3151, 3425.
71. *Diary,* 3489.
72. *Diary,* 2053, 3432, 3500.
73. *Diary,* 3325-6.
74. Evelyn Underhill, *Mysticism* (New York: Dutton, 1961) 176–9.

11

Experiential Theology
(1911-1919)

Having traveled with Fred Price on his spiritual journey and having experienced his unique life with Bernadette, we need to understand the theology lived during the journey in order to evaluate that experience. This chapter studies the spiritual experiences and relationships just discussed to develop the experiential theological statements concerning Bernadette as a saint, the Blessed Mother, Jesus, the Trinity, and marriage.

Bernadette Soubirous

Fred Price saw Bernadette as a beautiful woman, i.e., a woman of "ravishing beauty." The relationship was beyond the "knight and lady of the castle" image, with the lady being loved from afar by her knight who does great deeds of valor. She was his spouse, his one and only sweetheart for eternity both in desire and reality. Her presence with him was desperately needed; otherwise he would rather die. To Fred, Bernadette was a saint from the moment they met. He rejoiced as she moved up the formal Church ladder to sainthood. From the beginning she was his model; a model who was the purest, humblest, simplest, and most crucified and privileged. She was the purest of all virgins. She was his route to Jesus through poverty, humiliation, and the cross. She makes it possible for Fred to join Jesus on the cross. Unlike the Blessed Mother, she was not a matchmaker. Bernadette possessed him body and soul and was enthroned in his heart. She possessed him so much that he felt that she was alive in him:[1]

Again to-day and for some little time past, my difficulties about prayer to our Lord—direct—causing a sort of separation from my Bride seemed to have ceased and I have felt that Jesus and Mother never would allow us to be separated but that I should always approach and pray to Jesus and the most Holy Trinity through and as a part of my Bride she praying and absorbing me in her prayer for we are one being and this I feel all the time, so that when we say a prayer or psalm etc. She says it and speaks for us both we being as it were one being and I cannot explain this well but we speak and pray and act and feel as one being, I annihilated in her and this all the time and my life seems heaven on earth. I live [now] not I but Bernadette my Bride lives in me—we live—not we, Bernadette my Bride and I—but Jesus lives in us—that is our life, Mother, and I cannot better explain and it seems to me much heaven as heaven on earth can be.[2]

She was Fred's link with Jesus, the experience of the divine. She was totally dedicated to him, to being one with him, and living in him since the Blessed Mother united them. In the *Diary* she summarized her conduct towards Fred, her poor spouse:

I made it clear to my poor spouse that my whole conduct was to make him annihilated himself—to repress self—that I and Jesus might live in him, and I made him see that I had done this from the first day you made us one and that it must be so continuously and progressively (likely) throughout life and thus he is to love and seek after every positive occasion to deny and repress himself.[3]

Bernadette also revealed her own spirituality:

. . . in your mercy you caused me when he was kneeling at your feet at our home in our grotto at Lourdes—to be born into him— to take possession of him—as grace in baptism is born in the soul and takes of it, that you caused me to grow in him and take fuller possession of him until his consecration to me—then the years after our marriage—then you engaged us in marriage as one being to Jesus—then you gave us our eternal work through our grandmother, your mother, St. Anne, gradually leading to it by wonderful answer to prayers till on the last feast of St. Anne you gave it in explicitness—that you should grant us to be and my sweet heart and this should be our sole business—our sole occupation—our sole work—for all time and eternity.[4]

Their union was initiated by the Blessed Mother, and they were her special children and her slaves as represented by Fred's chains.[5] Bernadette was above all things, except the Blessed Mother and Jesus. Again the Blessed Mother was a catalyst for their union. It was Bernadette not the Blessed Mother that was Fred's heavenly vision:

> I filled him with me and with the greatest joy that he had me for his Bride and I was with him holding him in my possession more than ever!! . . . I am his ambition—I am now his unbridled heavenly vision.[6]

Bernadette was beautiful, ravishing. For Fred she had the virtues of purity, humility, and simplicity that he needed to emulate. She sought to annihilate his former vile self. She had a special closeness to the Blessed Mother and Jesus. The union between Fred and Bernadette was eternal. While Bernadette was the direct link to Jesus, the Blessed Mother played an important role in bringing Bernadette and Fred together and as a link to the Trinity.

The Blessed Mother

From the time the Blessed Mother pointed to the spar in the water during the Rebecca Clyde's floundering in 1887, she was Fred Price's guide. With the Blessed Mother he shared his daily life starting with the retreat of 1908. She was his source of grace and blessings. It was through the Blessed Mother that this type of communication with the divine took place:

> For a long time this sadness about Bernadette—all the afternoon—continued but it has settled in my mind that this position of Bernadette in the work—not to be seen so as [not] to overshadow the splendor of the Im[maculate] Conception—is what we both desire.[7]

She guided him, introduced him to Bernadette at Lourdes. He was extremely devoted to the Blessed Mother as her slave wearing her chains. She truly assumed the role of mother and benefactress to them. She gave Fred interior trials of purgation and directed Bernadette on how to deal with him. She was the source of Jesus' presence and his delight in the Trinity:

> To-day was filled with spiritual delights—almost ecstatic at times—in which I made my poor spouse realize as he had never done how Jesus and the Holy Trinity reside in you—that you are their created heaven—That as Jesus is in the Tabernacle, so He and the Holy Trinity are in you, you are their tabernacle [from] which the Divine Majesty flows upon His creatures and through whom or which they flow to the Divine Majesty—and we rejoiced with all our heart, Mother, almost in ecstasy in your greatness.[8]

Unfortunately, the special union between the Blessed Mother and Bernadette and Fred as a couple was not known because of the loss of the original notebook of the *Diary*. We only know of it through its being mentioned on the anniversary date.[9]

For Fred there was a definite hierarchy of persons moving from Bernadette to the Blessed Mother and then to Jesus. The grace flows via the Blessed Mother, but Bernadette was the direct link for Fred to life in Jesus. They were totally dedicated to her as their mother and guide, for she was Jesus' will. Through Bernadette's dedication to the Blessed Mother, she represented Jesus's will to Fred. The Blessed Mother made them one being.[10]

Christology

Until Jesus' presence was experienced mystically, Fred praised Jesus daily in the *Diary* and in celebrating Mass and praying the Divine Office, the Little Office of the Blessed Virgin, the Rosary, the Stations of the Cross, and other prayers before the tabernacle. Jesus' communication of his divine life to Bernadette and Fred was the source of their unity.[11] From 1912 on the letters of the *Diary* have a seal or handwritten monogram in the heading. Jesus is at the center of the seal with the words "through his mother and ours, M. B." or the words "through his and our mother, the Immaculate Conception and through Bernadette."[12]

Jesus' possession and transportation of Fred and Bernadette took place not in front of the tabernacle but in Fred's room and in the woods at their secret shrine. The indwelling of Jesus was directly related to the union with Bernadette, their marriage. Her linking Fred to Jesus in her, via the cross, was a deepening of Jesus' presence. The suffering Jesus was central to their experience of having their marriage completed in February 1917.[13] Jesus is also called "our Divine Spouse" in the *Diary*. Jesus' presence with the couple as his bride was often accompanied with the presence of the Holy Trinity.

Trinity

The entries in the *Diary* focus on the experience that Bernadette and Fred were having rather than on describing Jesus or the Trinity. They speak of resting in the Divine Majesty. The Holy Spirit, however, is described as coming with sweet unction:

> I make my poor spouse feel lost in me and we in the Blessed Trinity and we breathe our life in the Holy Trinity and we like heaven—inconceivable happiness. What is heaven and eternity but the fullness of and eternity of this! So it seems to my poor spouse whom I continuously inebriate with heavenly delights in me.[14]

Marriage

Fred's own conclusion concerning his marriage to Bernadette was that it was a mystical marriage, but instead of being married to Jesus, Fred was married to Bernadette. The marriage to Jesus by the couple is not questioned at all by Fred or Bernadette in the *Diary.*

In both cases marriage is the natural outcome of the growing spiritual relationship. The marriage ceremony and relationship that calls for a marriage was preceded by a consecration of Fred or Fred and Bernadette to the beloved. The marriage not only symbolized that the loving union had taken place but also that the spouses would continue to grow together as one being.

It is the Blessed Mother who made them one, yet Jesus is the source of the unity in the relationship.[15] For Fred the unity with Jesus by crucifixion is via Bernadette. This parallels the experience of Bernadette taking possession of Fred and then the presence of

Jesus. He takes possession of *them* as one. In him they experience the Trinity. This appears to be an experience of the inner communication of God. The experience of the divine (spouse and majesty) is by the individual but beyond the individual and within the marriage relationship.

FIGURE #3

"The Couple and Jesus"

Fred follows a heterosexual path to union with the divine. His natural attraction to women is clear from his struggle to avoid their beauty so that he would remain faithful to Bernadette. The mystical marriages moves Fred through union with the feminine who is in union with the divine, Jesus. Complete and total union, body and soul, with the divine via Jesus is achieved without having to seek union through the soul only. The union is total, body and soul, and maintains the anthropological integrity of the individual. The marriage union is then the ultimate relationship yielding the divine Presence when the couple is mutually and totally committed to giving selflessly to each other.

Fred's spiritual journey, with its leadership by the Blessed Mother, spiritual relationship with a deceased woman not yet formally recognized by the Church as a saint, and their subsequent marriage to Jesus and the experience of God's Presence allows Fred to achieve the objective of the spiritual quest via his cultural understanding and without surrendering his identity as a gentleman. All of this makes Thomas Frederick Price a unique figure in Christian spiritual tradition.

Notes

1. *Diary,* 1077, 1233, 1433, 1572, 1861–2, 1878, 1987, 2439, 2508, 2511, 2535, 2559, 2650.

2. *Diary,* 1787.
3. *Diary,* 3328.
4. *Diary,* 2304.
5. *Diary,* 2087, 2635.
6. *Diary,* 2730.
7. *Diary,* 1440.
8. *Diary,* 2242.
9. *Diary* mentions the anniversary on July 2, 1918 and 1919. *Diary* 3126, 3483.
10. *Diary,* 2098.
11. *Diary,* 1143.
12. *Diary,* 795–1497, 1496–3534.
13. *Diary,* 2842–2921.
14. *Diary,* 2346.
15. *Diary,* 1677, 1151.

12

Theological Comparison

Two Theologies

As we saw earlier, Fred in developing his expressional theology was trying to represent the teachings of the Church within his own cultural context. This expressional understanding from chapter 7 can now be compared with the experiential theology as summarized in the last chapter to see if there is a transcendence to his spiritual experiences.

Saints and the Blessed Mother

The expressional theological position that prayer to Jesus, God, was to be funneled through the saints, especially the Blessed Mother, was dramatically experienced by Fred in the SS Rebecca Clyde event. Fred Price's calling for Jesus' help and seeing the Blessed Mother could not have been a better reenforcement. This pattern of going to Jesus through the saints is maintained in Fred's relationship with Bernadette.

Fred did not have much trouble with the Marian approach to the spiritual life until Father Vieban's talk at St. Mary's Seminary in 1912. Crucial to that issue was the indwelling of the Trinity in the Blessed Mother. While the acceptability of Marian prayer as trinitarian was reenforced by Father Chapon, the spiritual experience of the Trinity is found in Fred's union with Bernadette.

Fred would always return to the ascending hierarchy of Bernadette, the Blessed Mother and Jesus, God. The experience of Jesus and the divine was via Bernadette and only a few times was it noted that the Blessed Mother was present. This indicates that there existed in the realm of experience routes to communicate with Jesus that were other than through the Blessed Mother. However, since the Blessed Mother introduced the couple to each other, one could claim that their entire relationship was through the Blessed Mother. Certainly Fred believed that the Blessed Mother directly controls divine grace.

As the *Diary* is taken over by Bernadette, it is obvious that the personal focus for Fred shifts from the Blessed Mother to Bernadette. Yet there is still the daily letter, the prayer for help and assistance, and the mission of proclaiming the Immaculate Conception. The saints' role as an intermediary (kinkeeper) in the expressional theology is preserved in the experiential theology; the position of the Blessed Mother as the most powerful intercessor is fully maintained. It is in the experience of "union with Bernadette" that the route to the divine deviates from a pure Marian path.

Marriage and Women

The spiritual marriage fulfilled for Fred and Bernadette the expressional theology of the loving union of the couple in Christ. The sacramental rites performed for their wedding stated their understanding of their type of union. The union of the two was the first and only issue during their marriage. The only children mentioned in the *Diary* were those of an orphanage in France. Children were not the focal point in the expressional theology of marriage. The concept of being faithful to each other was more important than the idea of procreating children.

Faithfulness is the expressional key to the marriage. It is experientially shown in Fred's fighting off temptations that would seduce him away from total commitment to Bernadette. Other women were a temptation to Fred. The expressional theology stated that "the role of men was to make women sacred." This possibly could be seen in Fred's desire to drive immodest women from church or to refuse them Communion. However, even he recognized that his standards of immodesty were different from that of society. His reaction to women was to withdraw, practice mortification and ask the Blessed Mother for assistance as the expressional theology taught. Clearly it is not Fred who makes Bernadette sacred. It is she who purifies him. She is his salvation. Here the experience does *not* parallel the expressional theology. Spiritually it is the woman who sanctifies. This is the same as Southern culture, where the woman is to be the personification of virtue.

However, it is also important to note that in order to enjoy the fruits of union it takes both of them. The expressional theology tells us that as a sacramental couple they are in union with Christ, and this is exactly what Fred and Bernadette experienced. Still it is through the saint (Bernadette) that he is able to experience Jesus and the Trinity.

Christology

The expressional Christology limited the locus of Jesus Christ to two places. One was the right hand of the Father in heaven and the other was his presence in the Eucharist. Fred believed in the divine Presence in the Eucharist for he would spend long hours in prayer before the tabernacle. However, the experience of Jesus himself in the midst of Fred and Bernadette in loving ecstasy was at locations other than in front of the tabernacle or during the consecration at Mass. Christ was experienced in Fred's room, at shrines, and during the Stations of the Cross. The experienced Christology goes far beyond the expressional statements.

The experience of Jesus for Bernadette and Fred leads to that of the Trinity. They saw Jesus as their divine spouse and as part of the divine Presence, which indicates that they experienced him as part of the Trinity. This parallels the expressional theological position that Jesus is the second person of the Trinity.

Trinity

Unfortunately Fred wrote little about the Trinity. A few references do exist to the Holy Spirit, but there are none about the Father. Both expressional and experiential theologies appear to have had a trinitarian base that is expressionally assumed and experientially expected. The de Montfort explanation of the Trinity in Marian prayer offered by Father Chapon was quite acceptable to Fred.

Transcendence

In his concern over the properness of prayer and relationships, Fred followed the Church's teaching in his spiritual life. However, the experiential theology goes beyond the expressional theology in the area of Christology with Jesus' presence outside of heaven and the Eucharist. In the relationship between men and women, the expressional understanding seems to be contrary to the experience of the woman as the purifier of the male, as Bernadette did for Fred. His spiritual and theological training were both a hindrance and a foundation for Fred's experience at Lourdes. However at the same time they were not a projection of this training. We can conclude that his spiritual experience transcended his learned spirituality and theology.

13

Transcendent Reflections

Fred's experience of the Blessed Mother and Bernadette opened new areas of spiritual experiences. These experiences raise psychological questions concerning the type of relationships Fred had with the Blessed Mother and his beloved Bernadette. The possibility that the relationship with Bernadette was a projection of prior understandings and/or desires and whether or not that was a normal male-female relationship must be considered.

The Blessed Mother

It would have been easy for Fred to fully accept the Blessed Mother as his mother after the healing of Father Moore, the vision by his nephew, and the healing of his deafness in 1886-1887. The sinking of the Clyde and Fred Price's ending up on the beach even though he could not swim have been well established.

What is important to note about the experience is that in praying to Jesus he had a vision of the Blessed Mother. This was not a mystical conversion but a psychological acceptance of the Blessed Mother as the spiritual mother who guides him and to whom he gave praise and honor. The events concerning the Blessed Mother were reinforced by the dogmatic theology in Fred's life, but they are not psychological projections from the past. His relationship with the Blessed Mother filled some of the psychological void of female relationships and the kinkeeper in his life because of his celibacy and the death of his mother Clarissa.

Bernadette

At Lourdes there is no indication that in his prayer or prior expectations that Fred was projecting a spiritual relationship. In fact, he had only minimal knowledge about Bernadette before the visit. The initial experience at Lourdes does not appear to be a product of wishful projection or expectation of Bernadette. Still the experience of Bernadette after so much soul searching was for Fred real and valid. He naturally approached her as any good southern gentleman would approach a magnificent woman to whom he had been attracted. Father Chapon saw this relationship as one of a knight to the lady of the castle. It appears that he was projecting a platonic relationship as the knight went forth on his great lady's quest. This was an incomplete understanding of the chivalry tradition and of the southern culture. As their relationship became more intimate, Father Chapon also approved. If the Jungian analysis of the lady-of-the-castle tradition is correct, the lady is a projection of the anima and an idealized figure of a virgin.[1] This parallels Chapon's initial reaction to the relationship. He later realized that the relationship with Bernadette was more than a figure that was being idealized from afar. Chapon then encouraged Fred to seek parallels within the love tradition of the spiritual marriage. Fred as a southerner naturally saw the Lady of the Castle as his bride.

Fred certainly became Bernadette's unworthy knight who was intimately in love with her and would crusade for her causes by proclaiming the Immaculate Conception and praying for sinners. She came into his life as someone who loved him and who was dedicated to the Blessed Mother. The love and attention poured out to Bernadette did not decrease Fred's dedication to the Blessed Mother. On the contrary Mary actually becomes *their* Blessed Mother. He channeled his natural need for a personal relationship with a woman towards Bernadette, the beloved that the Blessed Mother had given him.

The relationship with Bernadette also fulfilled the natural desire for a male-female relationship. Fred's physical and psychological attraction to women was negatively expressed in his seeing women, especially attractive ones, as a distraction to his celibacy. With his introduction to Bernadette they became a severe distraction to that relationship. Fred actively pursued a life of dedication, loving and serving Bernadette in an exchange of total giving and receiving. The drive to give of oneself to another initially looks or feels as if it is termination. However, in this type of annihilation the self is actually expanded to include the other while not losing the self. This is the union of differences, a creative union, that intensifies the individual. It is a complementary union of opposites.[2] This is what Fred has described in his becoming one with Bernadette and their becoming one with Jesus.

Bernadette is described by Fred as the most pure, simple and humble. This to some extent parallels Jung's concept that a male's ideal woman is a projection of his anima from the unconscious. The relationship between them can also be seen as the fulfillment of both Bernadette and Fred. She provides the female image of purity, simplicity, and beauty to him, and he provides the active proclamation of his love for her and actively takes up her proclamation of the Immaculate Conception. He thereby provides anima and animus fulfillment for both of them on the conscious and unconscious levels. This is similar to the union of the self when it recognizes its conscious and unconscious levels.[3]

The relationship between Fred and Bernadette, their being a loving couple, was an act of giving life to human existence. Jungian thought shows the union of the two as complementary, a fitting together of the male and female parts of two individuals. As individuals they could be called incomplete or out of total balance; as a couple they moved towards being a complete whole and forming one being through self-transcendence. This psychological understanding of the love relationship provides a backdrop for the placing of Fred's spirituality within the Christian spiritual tradition.

Notes

1. C. G. Jung et al., *Man and His Symbols* (New York: Dell, 1964) 196.
2. Ewert H. Cousins, *Bonaventure*, 20.
3. C. G. Jung, *Psyche and Symbol*, 12.

14

Experiential Theological Comparison

In this chapter Fred's spirituality is discussed within the greater context of Judeo-Christian spiritual tradition. Fred's experiential theological model will be compared to the experiential theology of St. Francis of Assisi, specifically his relationship with Lady Poverty. This comparison provides a general evaluation of Fred's experience in light of a long-accepted spiritual tradition. After discussing the criteria for using St. Francis as the point of comparison, a model of his relationship with Lady Poverty will be constructed, and that will be compared with Fred's relationship with Bernadette.

The Spiritual-Love Tradition

The spiritual-love tradition within the Judeo-Christian religious experience dates back to the statement in Genesis 1:27 that humans were created male and female and that the union of the two was the image of God.[1] Within the Hebrew Scriptures the love tradition finds a focal point in the Song of Songs, which intimately and vividly expresses God's love for his people as a marriage union between the bridegroom and his bride. In addition to the prophetic expression of this loving union as seen in Hosea and Isaiah, this understanding of the Canticle tradition again became universally accepted in the period between the Jewish revolts against Rome, A.D. 70–132. The importance of the love relationship can be seen in the Rabbis' statement: "Had not the Torah been given, Canticles would have sufficed to guide the world."[2]

In the Christian Scriptures John the Baptist states that Jesus is the bridegroom (John 3:22-30), and Jesus himself proclaims to the Jews that he is the bridegroom in Mark's Gospel (2:18-19) and to the Samaritans in John's (4:1-42). In Matthew's Gospel Jesus uses parables of the bridegroom and the wedding feast to explain who he is (25:1-13; 22:1-14).

The image of Jesus as the bridegroom in the Song of Songs was used by Christian writers throughout the centuries. The first known commentary making such a point was written by Hippolytus of Rome around A.D. 200. Many commentaries were written between the third and the seventh centuries, including those of Origin, Athanasius of Alexandria, Gregory of Nyssa, Philo of Capasia, Jerome, Theodore of Mopsuestia, Polychronius, Jovinian, Theodoret of Cyrus, Cyril of Alexandria, Justus of Urgel, Casiodores, Gregory the Great, Isidore of Seville, and Aponius.[3]

One commentator, however, stands out from the rest because of his positive approach to marriage, sexuality and divine union and literal interpretation of the Song of Songs. He was Jovinian, an ascetic itinerant preacher, who was well versed in the Scriptures. It appears that his commentary was so positive towards marriage that he was in conflict with the Manichaen tendencies of the time. When he suggested that marriage was not subordinate to celibacy and other controversial understandings, he was rebuked by church authorities in Rome, Milan, and Hippo. About the same time that Jovinian was being attacked in the West (A.D. 390), Theodore, bishop of Mopsuestia, was attacked in the Eastern Church for his literal reading of the Canticle.[4]

After the sixth century only a few paraphrasings of earlier commentaries were attempted. It was not until the emergence of a society that perceived human love, sexuality, and marriage as good in the twelfth century that the Song of Songs and Jesus as the bridegroom were proclaimed with great vigor. (See Anslem of Laon, Hevre of Dol, Marbod of Remus, Richard of St. Victor, Rupert Abbot of Deutz, Harvena Abbot of Bona Spes in Hainault, Irimbert Abbot of Ambden).[5] This flowering of love was a major shift not only in the Christian secular and religious societies but also in Judaism, Islam, Hinduism, and Buddhism about the same time. This change was not temporary or minor.[6] The magnitude of the blooming of this love tradition can be seen in the impact that it had on Fred's life as a Southern gentleman eight centuries later.

In the twelfth century a change occurred in monasticism with the founding of new Orders. They were different from the older Orders that had emerged a century after Jovinian's time in that they were made up of men and women who joined as adults. Many of the members of these new monastic organizations were nobles or knights who had been a part of the courtly culture of the castle. The influx of people who had lived in the secular society were bound together in their new society by a love of God. All were familiar with the secular love tradition and the concepts of courtly love, chivalry and the lady of the castle. The love experience was reflected in their writings.

This new approach to love was expressed by Bernard of Clairvaux, who was a knight, monk, abbot, preacher, poet, and author.[7] The most famous of his works is the *Sermons on the Song of Songs,* the great love poems of Scripture that intimately express the love of God for his people as that of a bridegroom and bride.[8]

Bernard used the Song of Songs to explain the relationship between the monk's soul and God.[9] In his commentary he used the military and courtly language of the day to describe an aggressive monastic life to his monks. As Christ's militia the weapons they were to use were patience, humility and charity.[10] The passion for love as expressed in the troubadour's romantic songs was woven into his work as well:

> The remarkable thing about these romances is that they sang not so much of love man for women—though, love-making is to some extent present in them—as of tournaments, jousts, and all kinds of military adventures. They very frequently tell of the winning of a beloved lady's hand by great arduous feats of knightly valour or of a knight proving his love for his lady by marvelous deeds of courage.[11]

Bernard uses biblical images within the twelfth-century love context to describe "the intimate union of Church with her King, as well as of the union of the individual soul with her Lord in the

Church and monastic life."[12] There was a channeling of the aggressive and romantic spirit of secular society into the field of religious experience. This allowed for a complete integration of a monk's life and gave him a choice of options in using his human desires to seek the absolute value of the love of God and to shift the focus of his concentration away from the self to Christ.

There is also an important insight for the monks who would not be interested in loving the male image of Christ directly. That also is in his *Sermons on the Song of Songs*. Bernard describes the mystical union between Christ, the bridegroom, and the soul, the bride. Psychologically this saves the knight from a homosexual relationship and allows for a deep mystical union. In other words he takes the inward path to union with Christ via the inner psyche. In Jungian terms this might be expressed as the anima, the feminine dimension within the male, accepting union with Christ. The love experience is that of mutual giving and receiving via the inner path initiated by the love of the bridegroom whose "love requires of his bride nothing more than a return of love and loyalty."[13] This parallels the outward path love described in Freudian psychology of total giving and seeking union with the other. The coincidence of opposites, the anima and animus, within the individual allows for union via the soul with another of the same sex. The courtly love tradition produces another mystic who uses that tradition as a basis for seeking union with Christ, i.e., Francis of Assisi.

Selecting a Case for Comparison

In constructing the comparison it seems that the major spiritual sources that affected Fred's spiritual development would not be used for two reasons. They might prejudice the validity of the comparison, and the issue of how closely Fred followed that particular tradition would unnecessarily confuse the question. Therefore, neither the de Montfort understanding nor the Carmelite and Jesuit saints will be used for this study. To aid in the comparison a person of parallel cultural background, attitude towards poverty, ministerial achievements such as founding a religious society, extensive writings/publishing, involvement in a spiritual marriage, and devotion to the Blessed Mother would be helpful. Again in this type of study, the most powerful character-istic should strike a common chord—something that resonates within the human experience regardless of time or place is what will be used for comparison.

Certainly, except for the amount of personal writing, St. Francis of Assisi fits the above description. Of particular impor-tance is the fact that Fred did not use Francis as a guide and that there is no evidence that Fred had any meaningful contact with any of the Franciscan Orders. In addition, there is little mention of St. Francis in *Truth*.[14] In the *Diary* there are only two refer-ences to Francis. One was about Francis' love of simplicity and how Fred was not living a vow of poverty the way Francis did,[15] and the other was that Fred saw a parallel between the terrible purgation and purification that took place at Lourdes in 1912 before his consecration to Bernadette and the purification and purgation that Francis suffered in getting his stigmata.[16] There is no indication that Fred thought about Lady Poverty. Certainly he would have investigated the situation had he thought it paralleled his own relationship with Bernadette, or he would have mentioned, as he did other times, that pursuing a study of Lady Poverty would be a distraction to his relationship with Bernadette.

Even though these men were centuries apart, it is interesting to note the similarities in their particular cultural settings. They are both from the knightly, courtly tradition of chivalry within their own cultures and centuries.[17] They both made major contri-butions to the development of religious Orders within the Church.[18] Both men were religious celibates within Catholic tra-dition. They had dynamic, dramatic beginnings to their spiritual lives (St. Francis hearing the voices and Fred seeing the Blessed Mother in the water off the North Carolina coast).

While there are major similarities, beyond the fact that these men lived seven centuries apart, there are other major differences. Francis' cultural roots were Italian with most of his life spent in Italy. Fred's origins were Southern English American, but the years of spiritual interest to us were spent in the northeastern United States and China. The most significant difference, how-ever, is the fact that the type of source material for understanding each man's journey is not the same. Fred left us the *Diary*, while the Franciscan tradition gives us images of Lady Poverty. A direct literary comparison of a diary or spiritual letters is not possible. Fortunately, the images of Lady Poverty are so strong that the character roles are identifiable in the various texts, making the construction of an experiential model possible.

Even with these differences, Francis represents for us a classic example of transcendence through love and therefore is an excellent point of comparison to Fred. Francis' love relationship with Lady Poverty is well known and an important part of Franciscan spirituality. The approach to the study of the relationship, then, is to establish the Franciscan source material to be used and then analyze the relationship.

Finding Francis' Lady Poverty

Lady Poverty was an important figure in the life of St. Francis of Assisi. However, to ask the role of Lady Poverty in the spirituality of Francis requires asking: Who was Lady Poverty *to* Francis? This question is further complicated by the fact that there was a tension in the Order of Friars Minor between those who wanted to follow a strict rule of poverty, later called the "spirituals," and those who recognized the need to have some funding for the Order because of its size.[19] This rift is reflected in the biographies of Francis.[20] Even in the "non-spiritual" tradition, Francis' devotion to poverty could not be hidden.[21] In a later biography, St. Bonaventure, taking a middle position in the debate over poverty,[22] still devotes a chapter to "Francis' Love of Poverty."[23] This devotion is definitely woven into the Rules of the Order written by Francis himself.[24]

During the last years of his life, Francis wrote in his *Testament* about upholding personal poverty: "The friars must be careful not to accept churches or poor dwellings for themselves, or anything else for themselves, unless they are in harmony with poverty which we have promised in the rule; and they should occupy these places only as strangers and pilgrims."[25] In the *Praises of the Virtues,* attributed to Francis, Wisdom is personified as the Queen of Virtues and Poverty has the title "Holy Lady."[26]

Finally, in a work dated shortly after Francis' death, the *Sacrum commercium Sancti Francisci cum Domina paupertate,*[27] we have an account of the relationship between Lady Poverty and Francis written in the style of the courtly epic.[28] This type of writing was popular in the culture from which Francis and his followers came. This work is definitely part of the Franciscan tradition and is accepted as an accurate portrayal of his relationship with Lady Poverty.[29]

To understand the role of Lady Poverty in Francis' spiritual life, or rather who she is to him, the following key works will be used: from the early period of historical writings, the *Sacrum commercium Sancti Francisci cum Domina paupertate,* from the second period, Thomas Celano's *Second Life,* and from the middle of the thirteenth century, Bonaventure's *Major Life.* In addition to the works mentioned above, there is a considerable amount of literature on Francis. These writings, however, either duplicate or are duplicated in the sources we will use[30] or are later period writings that were embroiled in the controversy between the moderates, Franciscans who held poverty in name only, and the spirituals who, by the 1300s had drifted off towards Joachimism.[31] Sources from these categories will not be used.

Lady Poverty

In the various sources Francis begins to relate to Poverty as if she were a real person in his life. Bonaventure links Francis' life and his personification of the experience and points out how Francis loved poverty: "He was eager to espouse it in everlasting love." Francis left everything and gave up everything for it, this marriage of eternal love.[32] He said that poverty was a special way to salvation.[33] She is the way and one follows this way by only seeking poverty and not other things. It is poverty that ends in nakedness with Jesus.[34] The change in Francis' view of the world can be seen in his realizing that in poverty there is abundance, all that one needs.[35] Francis rejoiced when he was addressed as "Lady Poverty" marking the oneness of the union with her as seen by others.[36] Bonaventure gives us further insight into the personal relationship and how much poverty was, over all else, first for Francis as he lived:

> in poverty, chastity and
> obedience shone forth

> all perfectly equal in
>   the man of God
> although he had chosen
>   to glory above all in
>   the privilege of poverty
>   which he used to call
>   his mother, his bride, his lady[37]

There is no doubt that Francis saw poverty primarily as his lady.[38]

Thomas of Celano, as Bonaventure, was interested in the person of Francis; therefore, the characteristics of the Lady are less accentuated. This point of view is very helpful for it gives us a clear picture of Francis. Thomas says that Francis "sought to espouse" poverty and, loving her beauty, he left all to seek her.[39] He considered a poor bed of straw to be their wedding bed.[40] The marriage bond with Lady Poverty is an indissoluble bond, an everlasting union, the two of them as one spirit. She is patient, will not perish, and rejoices.[41] Francis has chosen the way of poverty out of love for Jesus; the Lord is well pleased with voluntary poverty.[42] Finally, he requests that his naked body be placed on the ground to die, a sign of total poverty.[43]

A picture of Lady Poverty as the way and the guide emerges as Francis moves up the mountain of spiritual assent and experiences her comfort and peace. For Francis and his brothers, Poverty is the way to the Lord; they will walk in her path; she will teach them the way.[44] The Wisdom of the Lord makes her beautiful. While she seeks union, she is led into the bridal chamber, is filled with joy by the groom's offer, and is faithful to it. As the bride, she is the vessel through which they will enter the eternal kingdom.[45]

From this summary, Lady Poverty's characteristics can be listed: She is beautiful. She accepts freely his offer to dwell in him. In return she is to him: wisdom, patience, peace and comfort. She is naked and he will join her. She is persecuted. She is loved by Christ, and she is exalted by him. She is the vessel in which others must dwell to reach him. She seeks union with her beloved and is faithful always in the everlasting union.

Finally, there is Francis' seeking out of his beloved as the widow of Christ—alone since his death.[46] The following image of the interrelationship emerges with Francis being united with Lady Poverty, the widow of Christ, and therefore sharing in her union with Jesus.[47]

FIGURE #4

Lady Poverty as the Vessel of Union

An important fourteenth-century, non-Franciscan source concerning Francis and Lady Poverty, namely, Dante in canto XI of the "Paradiso" of *The Divine Comedy,* presents Francis seeking out this widow of Christ. Dante is more dramatic in his use of the sensual language and, thereby, favors the romantic side of the love between romantic and courtly love. The presentation, however, reinforces our Franciscan picture of Lady Poverty being faithful and the one in whom Francis found joy and rest. Dante is an important indicator that the model that had been constructed above was widely accepted as representative of Francis and his Lady.[48]

In addition to the positive feminine image of Lady Poverty, the *Sacrum commercium* offers feminine rivals to Francis' beloved. These rivals are vices that are personified in negative images of corruption. These vices make men turn against Poverty. They are: avarice, who is characterized as wicked, unfeeling, cunning, immoderate and a seducer of men, and sloth, who is the one who decreases spiritual care and interest in salvation and brings on envy. The union of Christ and Lady Poverty is stressed in Francis' reaction to these other women. For Francis, rejecting poverty is the same as rejecting the Lord.[49]

This negative image aside, we can see the love of Francis for Lady Poverty. Certainly the indwelling of each in the other and the seeking of union and espousing language implies a marriage in Christ. While Lady Poverty is not a living human being, she is the way to Christ and Francis acts out his love for her in a real way throughout his life up to and including his death. If there is a difference between romantic and courtly love, Francis appears to move from the courtly love with its knightly dedication to what is an intimate union, the ultimate union, with his Lady as he dies.

Comparing the Couples

Certain important similarities exist between Fred and Bernadette's relationship and that of St. Francis and Lady Poverty's. The most striking parallel is that within the marriage the male celibate moves through union with his bride to union with Jesus on the cross.

Lady Poverty is the personification of poverty to Francis, and she is the crucified widow of Jesus on the cross. By joining Lady Poverty, Francis achieves union with Christ. Bernadette was the model of poverty to Fred, the most pure virgin, and the cross for Fred. Both women were beautiful to their lover, and they brought joy, peace and happiness to them. Both men are tempted by the world around them in a real way. Such temptations expressed as vices in the *Sacrum commercium* for Francis and as vices, real people and situations, in Fred's *Diary*. While Francis needs to avoid avarice and sloth, Fred fights against pride and ambition. He is being seduced by other women and spiritual relationships that would otherwise be encouraged and considered good. Both men struggle to be faithful and not to be distracted from their beloved. They were in need of the ladies to succeed in their spiritual life. To be without their Lady was to lead a life not worth living. Bernadette and Lady Poverty dwelt within their lovers, yielding a marriage union whose fruits were a union with Jesus.

Marriage

The marriage between a man and a woman is the relationship that is the context for Fred and Bernadette to experience each other and to experience Jesus. It is in knowing Bernadette that Fred has a tangible understanding of virtues of poverty, humility, and simplicity. For St. Francis a marriage relationship emerges from acting out the virtue, and it is within this context that he experiences the Lord. Fred's experience is definitely that of a person, Bernadette, who to him personifies the virtuous qualities but Francis's experience is with a virtue, poverty.

Certainly the parallels between Fred's spiritual journey and Francis' life are striking. Fred goes beyond the Franciscan tradition of love of virtue to love of a person, a member of the Church triumphant in heaven. For Francis it is the union with Lady Poverty, who is in union with Jesus, that yields the saint's union with Christ; it is as one being that Fred and Bernadette experience union with Christ. Jesus comes to them together in their coupleness. However Lady Poverty already has a union with Jesus and therefore Francis' union with Christ is *through* her. Fred experiences Jesus *as one with* Bernadette.

In Fred's and Bernadette's relationship the coincidence of opposites yields transcending experiences of God. These experiences appear not to be projections from previous teachings, though they are founded in courtly love.

The relationships experienced by Fred were certainly within the cultural framework understandable to a southerner. Yet they are non-projected experiences for Fred's experiential theology goes beyond the expressed one as well as transcending Francis' experience. Fred Price and Bernadette Soubirous have opened new ground for the Canticle tradition.

Notes

1. Bruce Vawter, *On Genesis: A New Reading* (Garden City, N.Y.: Doubleday, 1977) 25, 55–60; Raymond Brown, et al, *The Jerome Biblical Commentaries* (Englewood Cliffs, N.J.: Prentice-Hall, 1968) 11; Phyllis Trible, *God and the Rhetoric of Sexuality* (Philadelphia: Fortress, 1978) 12–23; Pierre Grelot, *Man and Wife in Scripture* (New York: Herder, 1964) 36.

2. Marvin H. Pope, *Song of Songs* (Garden City, N.Y.: Doubleday, 1977) 92.

3. Pope, *Song of Songs,* 114–22.

4. Pope, *Song of Songs,* 119–20.

5. Pope, *Song of Songs,* 122–3.

6. Ewert H. Cousins, "Preface" to *Bernard of Clairvaux,* G. R. Evans, trans., introduction by Jean LeClercq (New York: Paulist, 1987) 6–9.

7. Jean LeClercq, *Monks and Love in Twelfth Century France* (New York: Oxford, 1979) 16–23.

8. LeClercq, *Monks and Love,* 9–16.

9. Bernard of Clairvaux, *On the Song of Songs I,* vol. 2 of *The Works of Bernard of Clairvaux,* Kilian Walsh, trans. (Kalamazoo: Cistercian, 1979) 2–3.

10. LeClercq, *Monks and Love,* 91–6.

11. LeClercq, *Monks and Love,* 99–100.

12. LeClercq, *Monks and Love,* 102–3.

13. LeClercq, *Monks and Love,* 128.

14. *Truth* 14:11 (November 1910) 342–5 and 2:1 (April 1898) 7–9.

15. *Diary,* 1943.

16. *Diary,* 1192.

17. Joan M. Erikson, *Saint Francis and His Four Ladies* (New York: Norton, 1970) 56-9, and see chapter 2 on Southern Culture.

18. See Jean LeClercq, Francis Vandenbrouche, and Louis Bouyer, *The Spirituality of the Middle Ages* (New York: Desclee 1968) 263–4, and Father Price's role in founding Maryknoll.

19. LeClercq et al., *The Spirituality of the Middle Ages,* 286–7.

20. LeClercq et al., *The Spirituality of the Middle Ages,* 289–99.

21. Thomas of Celano, *St. Francis of Assisi,* trans. and introduction by Placid Hermann (Chicago: Franciscan Herald, 1933) 15–7, 21, 37, 40–2, 68–9. These references are from the first life of St. Francis written in 1228-9 (ibid., xxv). The *Second Life* of St. Francis by Thomas better reflects the spirituality of Francis. This was written several years later—1244–6 (ibid., xxx).

22. Domien Vorreux, "Introduction to the Lives of St. Francis by Bonaventure" in *St. Francis of Assisi: Writings and Early Biographies, English Omnibus of the Sources for the Life of St. Francis,* Marion Habig, ed., Ralph Brown, Benen Fahy, Placid Hermann, Paul Oligny, Nesta de Robeck, Leo Sherely-Price, John R. H. Moorman, trans. Research bibliography by R. Brown (Chicago: Franciscan Herald, 1973) 617–23.

23. Bonaventure, *The Soul's Journey into God, The Tree of Life, The Life of St. Francis,* translation and introduction by Ewert Cousins, Preface by Ignatius Brady (New York: Paulist, 1978) 239–44.

24. Francis of Assisi, "The Rule of 1221, The Rule of 1223," in *Omnibus of Sources,* Benen Fahy, trans., 31–64. Of the 23 chapters in the Rule of 1221, 1, 2, 3, 7, 8, 9, 14, and 15 deal with poverty, and from the twelve chapters in the Rule of 1223, 1 through 6 discuss poverty.

25. Francis of Assisi, "The Praises of Virtue," *Omnibus of Sources,* Benen Fahy, trans., 132–4.

26. Francis of Assisi, "The Testament of Francis," *Omnibus of Sources*, Benen Fahy, trans., 68.

27. Placid Hermann, "Introduction to the Sacrum commercium," *Omnibus of Sources,* 1533–4.

28. Erikson, *Saint Francis and His Four Ladies,* 58–60, Placid Hermann, "Introduction to the Writings of St. Francis," *Omnibus of Sources,* 16–8.

29. Placid Hermann, "Introduction to the Sacrum commercium," *Omnibus of Sources,* 1539–46.

30. Theophile Desbonnets, "Introduction to the Legend of Perugia" in *Omnibus of Sources,* 969.

31. Raphael Brown, "Introduction to Little Flowers of St. Francis" in *Omnibus of Sources,* 1274–9.

32. Bonaventure, *The Life* (VII–1) 240.

33. Bonaventure, *The Life* (VII–1) 240; Thomas of Celano, *Saint Francis of Assisi* (55, 200) 185–6, 197.

34. Bonaventure, *The Life* (VII–2) 240–1.

35. Bonaventure, *The Life* (VII–10, 12, 13) 246–8.

36. Bonaventure, *The Life* (VII–6) 243, Thomas of Celano, *Saint Francis of Assisi* (93) 213–4.

37. Bonaventure, *The Life of Saint Francis* (VII–6) 244.

38. Saint Francis of Assisi, "The Praises of Virtue," *Omnibus of Sources*, 132.

39. Thomas of Celano, *Francis of Assisi* (55) 185–6.

40. Thomas of Celano, *Francis of Assisi* (63) 190.

41. Thomas of Celano, *Francis of Assisi* (70) 198.

42. Thomas of Celano, *Francis of Assisi* (73–4) 200.

43. Thomas of Celano, *Francis of Assisi* (217) 311.

44. "Sacrum commercium," *Omnibus of Sources,* Placid Hermann, trans., 1556–7.

45. "Sacrum commercium," 1556, 1561, 1563, 1573, 1585, 1586, 1589, 1596.

46. "Sacrum commercium," 1557.

47. "Sacrum commercium," 1594.

48. Dante Alighieri, *The Divine Comedy—Paradise,* translated by Dorothy L. Sayers and Barbara Reynolds, trans. (New York: Penguin, 1962) 149–56.

49. Dane Alighieri, *The Divine Comedy—Paradise,* 1576–85.

15

New Vistas in
Christian Spirituality

The objective of this study has been to describe and analyze the spirituality of Fr. Thomas Frederick Price of Maryknoll and his marriage to Sr. Bernadette Soubirous of Lourdes. So that the spirituality could be clearly identified and evaluated, archetypal models of both the expressive (or systematic) theology and the experiential theology (or spirituality) were presented by means of a seven-step methodology. This method not only allowed for the controlled use of several disciplines; it also required comparative critiques from theology, psychology, and spirituality within a cross-cultural context. By using this approach to spirituality, we have developed a picture of Fred Price's spiritual journey, experience, and expressive theology.

We have seen a man who was dedicated to the teachings of his Church, but whose experience of God and others went beyond that of the expressive theology. This was especially true in the areas of Christology, marriage, and women. The Jesus he experienced in the depth of his spiritual marriage to Bernadette was not restricted to heaven or the Eucharist. In his spiritual marriage he experienced a unity with Bernadette that was blessed with their mystical marriage to Jesus. Married couples are called to more than a life of faithfulness and caring for children. They are called to a life of intimate unity with each other and with God.

The women in Father Price's life were not morally or spiritually inferior to men. From Clarissa Bond Price, to the Blessed Mother, to Bernadette, they called Father Price to a deeper spiritual life. They were his guides and not a hindrance. Bernadette became the way he could achieve this life-long desire. She became his way to be one with Jesus. Certainly, Fred was not taught that this route was available. Yet it is a path open to married couples once sexuality is not looked upon as evil in and of itself.

The psychological comparison showed that Fred, through and with Bernadette, achieves a transcendence of self. There is between them a loving relationship of mutual giving and receiving, dedication to the Blessed Mother, and grounding in Christ. There can be little doubt that in Fred's reported experience he achieved an other-than-self focus through a loving relationship with Bernadette. This gave meaning to his life that is healthy from a psychological point of view.

Fred's journey represents a milestone in the history of spiritual relationships within the Christian tradition. His experience is an important development in the spiritual-love and mystical-marriage tradition. The tradition is expressed biblically in the Song of Songs and culturally flourished in the twelfth century. As we have seen above, Bernard of Clairvaux in his *Sermons on the Song of Songs* discusses the unity between a man's soul, as the bride of Christ, with God. In this approach to God, the soul parallels the feminine anima of the male's unconscious in the psyche and therefore preserves the masculinity of the individual seeking union with Christ. This is paralleled by the female saints such as Teresa of Avila who also experienced a mystical marriage directly with Jesus.

The next type of relationship is that of St. Francis and Lady Poverty where the male achieves union with Jesus through union with a feminine virtue that is united with him. In this case the female provides a link between the two males. With Fred Price and Bernadette Soubirous we have an example of the spiritual union between a living male and a female saint, a member of the Church triumphant. This marriage is of such a deep union that they, as one, experience a marriage with Jesus. This relationship goes beyond the Francis and Lady Poverty relationship in two ways. First, the relationship is between a living person and a person who had lived on earth rather than a personified virtue. Second, they, as a united couple, experience a mystical marriage to Jesus. Their experience of the presence of Jesus as divine Spouse is also important for it is a record of a couple experiencing the presence of Jesus as part of the sacramental encounter of marriage. The marriage experience was that of the complementary coincidence of opposites yielding transcendence as well as encounter with God. Marriage, then, is a route to unity with the divine for both the male and the female.

Based upon the criteria used in this study, we can conclude that Fred Price had a legitimate spiritual journey within the Christian-love tradition. His experience is an important link between celibate spirituality and married spirituality and opens wide new horizons for the development of an encounter spirituality for married couples.

Their Call to Us

Fred and Bernadette call us to look at the spiritual relationships between men and women in more depth than in the past. We need to take a fresh look at not only spiritual relationships such as Francis and Lady Poverty but also at celibate couples such as Catherine of Siena's spiritual and intimate relationship with Raymond of Capua[1] and Catherine of Genoa and Don Cattaneo Marabotto,[2] and Francis and Clare of Assisi.[3] All of these offer us a relationship worthy of study again.

Another type of relationship is the one in Dante's presentation of Beatrice in the *Divine Comedy*. Here we see a man whose inspiration is a woman who is married to another man. She is not only his guide but also "the embodiment of his love"[4] and his link with the divine. He realizes that

> the key to reality was somehow connected with that God-bearing image which was Beatrice, and yet not she, but which shone through and made her as the vision of God shines through and makes the vision of the universe. So now he searches the Godhead for sight of the Master-Image, the Reality of which Beatrice was the figure, that union of the Creator and created in the person of Christ.[5]

In addition to celibate couples, once married couples, and married (but not to each other) couples, Christian renewal programs of Marriage Encounter (a married couple communication

weekend) and Retorno (a prayer weekends for spouses) have encouraged spiritual reflection and growth of the couple as one.[6] All
of this calls for an understanding and spiritual life for Christians
beyond what has been dominant for centuries by celibate expressional and experiential theologies and a negative view of physical
sexual union.[7] We need to begin to see marriage as a path to
saintliness, women not as evil temptations but as evokers of good,
and the marriage union as a blessing from and route to God.[8]
Even if we do not fully understand, maybe we can begin to
experience humankind, a man and a woman naked and one flesh
(Gen 2:23-25), as the image of God (Gen 1:27).

Thus Fred and Bernadette are a part of the growth of western Christian spirituality. They have deepened our understanding
of union with one another and the divine and call us to study
married spirituality seriously. In spite of the ecclesial structures
and the expressive theology of the counter-reformation, a cultural
base of the Southern courtly love tradition helped produced a
married spirituality that reflects the biblical promise of Christ:
"For where two or three are gathered in my name, there am I in
the midst of them" (Matt 18:20).

Notes

1. Suzanne Noffke, "Introduction" to *Catherine of Siena, the
Dialogue* (New York: Paulist, 1980) 5-7.
2. Benedict J. Groeschel, "Introduction" to *Catherine of Genoa,
Purgation and Purgatory, the Spiritual Dialogue,* trans. and notes by Serge
Hughes (New York: Paulist, 1979) 16-7.
3. Thomas of Celano reports in *The Life of Saint Clare* that
Francis "was struck by the fair frame of so favored a maiden," and he
"visited Clare and she more often visited him" in the early stage of their
relationship (Thomas of Celano, *The Life of Saint Clare,* trans. and edited
by Paschal Robinson (Philadelphia: Dolphin, 1910) 10. Their relationship was spiritually intertwined and was beyond that of friends (Arnaldo
Fortini, *Francis of Assisi,* Helen Mark, trans., (New York: Crossroad,
1981) 357-60. See also Francis of Assisi and Clare of Assisi, *Francis and
Clare,* Regis J. Armstrong and Ignatius Brady, preface by John Vaughn,
Classics of Western Spirituality Series (New York: Paulist, 1982).
4. Barbara Reynolds, "Introduction," *The Divine Comedy—
Paradise* (New York: Penguin, 1962) 51.

5. Reynolds, "Introduction," 18.

6. An example of these emerging works is Tom and Lyn Scheuring's *Two for Joy* (New York: Paulist, 1976).

7. Augustine of Hippo with this use of Neo-Platonic thought has had a tremendous effect on Christian expressive and experiential theology since the fifth century. One of his key concepts that still affects both Roman and Reform thinking is the negative approach to physical sexuality (For a summary of this understanding see William C. Placher, *A History of Christian Theology* (Philadelphia: Westminster, 1983) 116–7.

8. Francis Younghusband, *Modern Mystics* (London: John Murray, 1935) 269–74.

Appendix A

Studying a Spirituality

The method needed in studying an individual's spirituality must not only identify the root of the unique transcendent experience using a multi-disciplinary approach but must also evaluate the experience. It must provide a means of accurately describing the situations and theologies being studied, enable us to compare the spiritual experience to other experiences and to systematic theologies, and establish criteria to evaluate the spiritual experience(s).

Currently academic discussions concerning how a spirituality can be analyzed focus on three approaches: phenomenological (also known as anthropological), historical, and theological.[1] Since all three are important to understand the totality of the spiritual experience, this study combines these approaches to both analyze the spiritual journey and critically evaluate the results.

The HISTORICAL APPROACH calls for not only placing the individual in the proper historical context or setting but also for critiquing the particular spirituality within the context of a theological (spiritual and dogmatic/doctrinal) tradition. The PHENOMENOLOGICAL APPROACH starts with the individual's experiences and calls for a critical analysis of the transcendence of the experience. Lastly, the THEOLOGICAL APPROACH requires construction of both the person's expressional (doctrinal or systematic) theology and experiential (spiritual) theology followed by a comparative examination of the two. Figure #5 shows how, by using the three approaches, we arrive at a SEVEN-STEP METHOD that has the THREE PHASES of (I) discovering (the analysis of the journey and experience), (II) extracting (the development of the expressional and experiential theologies), and

(III) evaluating the spirituality. The focal point of the analysis is (phase II; step 4) the experiential theology (the composite under- standing of the spiritual experience).

FIGURE #5

PHASES AND APPROACHES

Phase   Approach

I. DISCOVERING

Historical
[The Sources and Settings]

Phenomenological
[Journey and Experience]

II. EXTRACTING

Theological
[The Expressive Theology]
[The Experiential Theology]

III. EVALUATING

Theological
[Theological Comparison]

Phenomenological
[Transcendent Evaluation]

Historical
[Setting In the Tradition]

CONCLUSIONS

The Seven-Step Method

Needless to say, the demands of analyzing any spiritual journey or experience require a multi-disciplinary approach. However, the other disciplines such as psychology, sociology, history, philosophy, theology, anthropology, etc. are supporting disciplines to spirituality.[2] The supporting disciplines help increase the accuracy of the facts used in the study, but the conclusion concerning the experiences must be based on the discipline and its criteria of judgment that specifically studies the phenomenon of the encounter with the transcendent, i.e., spirituality.

FIGURE #6

STEPS TO UNDERSTANDING

Phase   STEP   Approach

I. DISCOVERING

Historical

STEP 1 *The Setting and Sources*
    1a The Cultural Setting
    1b The Sources

Phenomenological

STEP 2 *Journey and Experience*
    2a The Foundations
    2b The Development

II. EXTRACTING

Theological

STEP 3 *The Expressive Theology*

STEP 4 *The Experiential Theology*

III. EVALUATING

Theological

STEP 5 *Theological Comparison*

Phenomenological

STEP 6 *Transcendent Evaluation*

Historical

STEP 7 *Setting In the Tradition*

CONCLUSIONS

The key or primary criteria of the discipline of spirituality emerges from the subject matter itself—the criteria of transcendence. This deals with both transcendence of the self as well as the experience of a transcendent other. With this in mind, the following Seven Steps will be used to insure the proper development of key foundational understandings needed in doing the investigation and comparisons (See figure #6 for an overview of how each step corresponds to the phases of analysis).

PHASE I DISCOVERING

Steps 1 and 2
Cultural Background and Sources
Foundations and Developments

Step 1. *Understanding the Context and the Sources*
The first hurdle in understanding an individual's spirituality is to come to an accurate representation of both the situation and the meaning of the texts/documents that are available.[3]

Step 1a. *Determining the Cultural Setting.*
In doing a study that does not exactly conform to the researcher's and/or readers' culture, it is important to establish the cultural assumptions from which the various individuals being studied were working. In doing a spiritual analysis, it is important not only to do a secular and ecclesiastical setting but also present the theological and spiritual milieu in which the focus of the study was living. Even within one's own cultural frame, this type of study is required because it uncovers and states openly the underlying issues that might be missed if the cultural analysis were not undertaken. Determining the grand cultural setting will provide an essential backdrop for the proper understanding, use, and interpretation of the sources, events, and relationships in the case study.

Step 1b. *Examining the Sources.*
In most spirituality case studies, the data emerges from a variety of sources, which in turn usually come in different literary genres that were written at different times.

To begin to unlock this problem, each source must be looked at as a whole with an eye towards seeing the text from the author's point of view and motivation. In doing this we need to take into account the intended audience, historical setting (to especially include the liturgical, prayer and church setting), the literary genre, the sources used, and internal structure of the writing. This whole text point of view, or composition criticism, will keep us focused on the subject(s), authors and main characters, and on the theological, linguistical, and cultural settings in which each of the works was written.[4] Asher Finkel states that this method will allow us to determine the meaning of a text. The meaning to a text is "governed by the structural presentation of the surrounding material, is to be examined in view of the redactional arrangement, given stresses, added comments and specific terminology of the writer."[5]

Step 2. *Journey and Experience*

In this step we focus on the factors that led to embarking on the spiritual journey and the journey itself with its resulting spiritual experiences. In addition to looking for the specific threads that run through anyone's spiritual development, we will seek to identify the spiritual experiences. Both descriptive and analytical criteria will be used in analyzing the spiritual experiences.

Descriptive Criteria

It is important that criteria of judgment be applied in developing the theologies. We are faced with a problem very similar to the one that biblical scholars have when they seek the historical Jesus or try to construct the theology of a biblical author or editor. Fortunately they have developed several evaluative criteria that we can use. They are coherence, non-projection, multiple attestation, and compatibility.[6] The last one, compatibility, is used in phase 3: The Evaluation.

The criteria of *coherence* requires that an individual source must be consistent within itself. That is, the particular experiences (events and relationships) that a person reports must be consistent with each other.[7] Inconsistency would indicate that there could be problems concerning the accuracy of the report, the initial interpretation, or cultural analysis.

It is important that the experiences described by the individual not be projections of stories, pictures, or books to which he had been previously exposed. By using the criteria of *non-projection* we can eliminate events that are possibly imaginary or wishful thinking.[8]

Also, we will be looking for multiple attestation of an event, person, understanding, or relationship. Specifically, a description or idea expressed in different literary settings or that description or idea expressed by different individuals. This not only gives a better insight into the event, person, or thought but also provides an indicator of historicity and gives a clearer understanding.[9]

Analytical Criteria

In looking for truly transcendent, transforming experiences (also referred to as conversion experiences), analytical criteria are needed. This criteria emerge from the studies of deep religious experiences, mysticism, and ecstasy done by scholars such as Evelyn Underhill, James White, Marghanita Laski, etc.[10]

The criteria itself include a sense of liberation or victory, an awareness of the nearness and love of God, an out-pouring of love for God, a non-egocentric view of the individual's own life and actions, and love of others.[11] Other general characteristics of these experiences are that they defy adequate linguistic expression (ineffability), provide knowledge/truth beyond the intellectual (i.e., intuitive), give a deep core feeling of transcendence, and include a feeling of union with someone or something.[12]

Once the descriptive and analytical criteria have been used to determine the validity of the experiences, we can determine the stage or level of spiritual experience: conversion, purgation, illumination, surrender, and union.[13]

Step 2a. *Identifying the Foundations of the Theology and Spirituality.*

This will be done by developing a personal historical overview of the individual's life. This overview is *not* intended to be a complete biography; in Fred Price's case they have been written. The biographies, correspondence, and personal testimonies of those who knew him are used to present the key people, events, relationships, and places that shaped his missionary vision, theological understanding and spirituality. Such a portrait will provide a foundational understanding of the religious and spiritual traditions* for the interpretation of the dogmatic writings, spiritual journey, and spiritual events** from which the expressive and experiential models will be constructed.

Step 2b. *Understanding the Spiritual Development*
In this step the spiritual practices and forces that shaped the spirituality will be identified. This is an important step in specifically identifying experiential and expressional theology. It points to the path or paths upon which the individual is traveling helps determine the impact of events, relationships, religious teachings, and cultural settings upon the individual, and provides a reference for understanding the various experiences.

PHASE II EXTRACTING

Steps 3 and 4
The Expressive Theology
The Experiential Theology

This phase addresses the extraction of the expressive and experiential theologies so that they can be compared not only with themselves but with other material. To accomplish this an "archetype" approach*** to developing the grounds for comparison is

---

*Spiritual tradition refers to the experience, rules, and method of approaching prayer, actions, and beliefs as practiced by a church or religious community. Several religious or spiritual traditions made a significant impression on Fred Price. Some of them were the popular religious tradition in the Church in the southern United States and the tradition and writings of the Carmelites, the Society of Jesus, and the Marian devotions of Louis de Montfort.

**Spiritual Events are the key moments or times that are spiritual watersheds. These "spiritual events" are occasions that deepen a person's experiential understanding of God and the saints, and the actual encounters by a person with God or the saints. They encompass everything from a presence in prayer to visions and a deep mystical presence.

***The concept of using archetypal models in theological research was introduced by Ewert Cousins in an article entitled "Models and the

used to determine the expressional theology (or doctrinal statements) and the experiential theology based on the spiritual experiences.

The person's intellectual understanding is the expression of his/her concept of an item, person, or event. A Christian example of this would be Frederick Price's reply to questions concerning Jesus Christ, the Blessed Mother, or the Trinity in *Truth*. Contemporary examples would be Karl Rahner's *Theological Investigations* and Karl Barth's *Church Dogmatics*. This model or extract is also referred to as dogmatic, systematic or moral theology. This type of theology is *expressional;* however, in this study the expressional theology is not the true focal point.

The *experiential* theology is an individual's (or group's) experience of a spiritual event. An example of this would be an individual's description of an encounter with a person (e.g., Jesus Christ, the Blessed Mother, . . .) or event (out-of-body experiences, tongues, . . .). In other words we are dealing with two types of theology: one expressed and reflective or systematic, the other experienced and descriptive. Everyone has both expressional and experiential theologies by the fact that they are human. The challenge then is how to work with the two types of theology so that they can be compared and contrasted. This can be done by archetypal models, or composites of theological statements, which look to the core of the person.

By doing two theological models when a spirituality is analyzed, we then have two operative theologies—one being expressed in the individual's mind and the other experienced in the heart or core of his/her being. The two theologies act as a counter-balance to each other.

Step 3. *The Expressive Theology*

In determining the expressive theology the individual's doctrinal and systematic statements are gathered into a systematic theology. Where two different types of theological data are presented,

---

Future of Theology," *Continuum* (Winter-Spring, 1969) 82–7. A theological model or extract is the composite of theological statements concerning either an individual's (or group's) intellectual understanding or the individual's (or group's) experience of a spiritual event.

the modeling approach is very helpful. By a presentation of an individual's understanding on certain issues, one can then compare the findings with the theology being expressed by that individual at another time *or* experienced by her/him on the spiritual level. The theological issues to be modeled (extracted), are those key points that emerge from the individual's life, writings, and editings.

Step 4. *The Experiential Theology*

This is the heart of our study. In constructing the experiential theological model the most powerful characteristic should strike a common chord—something that resonates within the human experience regardless of time or place. These common experiences have been called archetypes.[14] In investigating archetype within a spiritual work, such as Father Price's spiritual *Diary,* it is both the experience from within the archetype as well as the experience of the archetype in the situation that reflects the true picture offered by the author. The archetype that emerges then is not abstract or removed. This is due to the fact that the model emerges from the experience while still in relationship to its surroundings, i.e., a grounding in reality. To remove either the experiential or expressional sides of the model would negate our ability to find the root or the touchstone with the common experience that the author's theologies might offer.

PHASE III EVALUATIONS

Steps 5, 6, and 7
Theological
Phenomenological
Historical

Evaluation by Comparison. The comparisons with a spirituality (experiential theology) as developed in step 4 should be done in three areas. First (step 5—Theological Approach) there is the comparison between the expressive and experiential theologies, next (step 6—The Phenomenological Approach) there is the need to look at the psychological reflections emerging from the spirituality, and finally (step 7—Historical Approach) there is the placement of the spiritual experience within the framework of the greater spiritual tradition and a comparison with another spirituality. Each comparison is important for it provides a specific critique of the spirituality in understanding, completeness/unity and continuity respectively.

The two key criteria used in this phase are transcendence and compatibility. The primary criteria of *transcendence* that emerges from the subject matter of spirituality itself, deals with transcendence beyond the self as well as the experience of a transcendent other. In addition as mentioned above in phase II, in doing the comparison we need to be aware of the criteria of *compatibility*. Compatibility with the historical tradition is especially important. In some way the personal spiritual experience should have a link within the spiritual tradition. To test the criteria of compatibility, comparison with historical, accepted figures in the tradition will be required. When compatibility is linked with the overriding criteria of transcendence then we are looking for the individual's experiences to emerge from the tradition but in their own right go beyond either what they had learned or what they had previously experienced.

Step 5. *Theological Comparison*

We begin with *the expressive-experiential comparison* which, in determining the similarities and differences, will identify changes, reveal points of conflict and indicate growth or stagnation in the theologies. This is an internal theological critique using the systematic theology to highlight the spiritual theology. In this study the specific areas of comparison between the theologies should cover the topics that have emerged from the studies in phase II.

Step 6. *The Phenomenological Comparison*

As mentioned above, specific to the study of a spirituality is the criteria of transcendence. Dealing with the transcendence of self can help us to establish an analytical method. Transcendence of self has long been taken seriously in psychology. This discipline can, therefore, be used to assist in the application of this criteria with regards to the individual and the inner life.

In this phenomenological comparison the mutual reflection between the spiritual journey and relationships and psychological theory will be sought. The focus will be on the transcendent nature of the journey and encounters.

Just as there has been a debate over the relationship between systematic theology and spirituality, there is a debate over the relationship between psychology and spirituality.[15] Currently the focus is on the relationship between the fields.[16] For the most part these psychoanalytical debates revolve around pathological issues rather than maturity issues in psychology and religion.[17] A psychoanalysis of the "subject individual" should *not* be the focus of our study because such an approach focuses on the problems not the results.[18] So, the pathological focus of the debate in the psycho-spiritual area should not be allowed to distract us from the objective of establishing the criteria of personal transcendence needed to evaluate a spiritual theology. The criteria of judgment needs to be rooted in the study of psychological maturity as opposed to the study of psychological deviations. The question being asked is not "why is a person not able to achieve transcendence?" but rather "what is personal transcendence?"

What is being sought is the resonance of the spirituality with the psychological understanding of human life that comes with a life of self-transcendence.[19] The criteria that emerges in this context can be stated as follows: Does the individual during his/her spiritual journey find wholeness, meaning and expansion, and an open horizon of love for another.

Personal transcendence as part of the journey to an ultimate reality is sometimes confused with self-integration which may or may not exist prior to the encounter with the divine. Also the experience of the blissful peace of the void is sometimes called a transcendent experience in both eastern and western psychology. However, this feeling is *not* a transcendent encounter involving total unity with the transcendent other.[20] Maslow's work on peak experiences outlined the characteristics of a wide variety of religious experiences. Many of them such as loss of fear, ego-transcendence, recognition of the experience as an end in itself, point to an experience of the ultimate reality.[21] Developing a criteria for a comparison with the experiential theology requires use of a psychological understanding based on relationships that emerge from the positive understanding of psychological life.

The writings of Carl G. Jung and Viktor E. Frankl are very helpful in defining the criteria.* Jung concentrated on the unconscious[22] and his major contribution in this area was the archetype. For Jung an archetype is the imprint or image of the instincts that are the dynamic energies in the unconscious.[23] The ego, in the conscious, contains the anima in females and the animus in males while in the unconscious, the shadow, has the contrasexual figure or the opposite sex archetype, i.e., the animus in the female or the anima in the male.[24] In the unity of the self, there is a dominant conscious animus and a subconscious anima in the male with the opposite existing in the female.[25] For the individual the internal unity of the self is not completely balanced. The unity of a man and a woman yields a union that creates a whole in which the animus and anima are in both the conscious and the unconscious. It is a unity of the coincidence of opposites. In this meeting the balance in the conscious selves and the unconscious selves moves to complete union beyond the one.

The union yields a transcendence of self and a differentiation of the individual. The union is of mutual complementary opposites; a unity that is an integration, ever intertwining, but still not obliterating either person.[26] Understanding the dynamic union of what appears to be but what is opposite is at the core of Jungian concepts of life and unity.[27] Victor Frankl expresses this as the actualization of the individual's potential in the act of self-transcendence by loving the beloved.[28] This *coincidence of opposites* gives life and vigor to the individual, creates an "us" that is one as well, and focuses on *transcending and the transcendent.* This understanding is used as the primary evaluating criteria of experiential theology. A secondary tool is that of the criteria of non-projection as mentioned above.

Step 7. *Comparison with the Spiritual Tradition*
The third area of evaluation is a historical comparison with the closest spiritual tradition or traditions to the spirituality of the

---

*Jung produced volumes of material. Some of these writings dealt with religion, God and/or Scripture. The conclusions concerning religion, though valuable, are not the focus of this study. Specifically we call on Jung to help us understand what is happening psychologically.

study. This comparison provides the critique of continuity, while we continue to look for transcendence. In other words we use the criteria of compatibility with the tradition. This can be done by placing the individual's spirituality in the context of the overall spiritual tradition, which in this study is the Christian tradition of love, and by comparing the spirituality to a specific example from the tradition. This establishes whether or not the individual's spirituality is congruent with or transcends that of the tradition.

These three phases and seven steps integrate the three areas of analysis (theological, phenomenological, and historical) into one method, a method that gives us not only a clear understanding of the cultural and religious premises that the subject is using and of the spiritual journey itself but also an evaluation of the experience. The conclusions of the study can be integrated into and used confidently in systematic, historical, or spirituality studies.

Notes

1. Douglas Burton-Christie, Keynote Address: "New Horizons in Spirituality," College Theological Society Annual Workshop, May 24, 1994. Bernard McGinn, "The Letter and the Spirit: Spirituality as an Academic Discipline" *Christian Spirituality Bulletin* 1:2 (Fall 1993) 1–10. Sandra M. Schneiders, "Spirituality as an Academic Discipline," *Christian Spirituality Bulletin* 1:2 (Fall 1993) 10–15. Walter H. Principe, "Broading the Focus: Context as Corrective Lens in Reading Historical Works in Spirituality," 1, 3–5; Bradley Hanson, "Theological Approaches to Spirituality, A Lutheran Perspective"; Sandra M. Schneiders, "A Hermeneutical Approach to the Study of Christian Spirituality," 9–14; *Christian Spirituality Bulletin* 2.1 (Spring 1994).

2. This is the approach used in the World Spirituality Series. See Cousins, "Preface to the Series."

3. While God being transcendent is beyond culture, certainly, humans are not. The communication between the two will in some way be effected by the cultural setting. See C. Philip Slate, "The Culture Concept and Hermeneutics: Quest to Identify the Permanent in Early Christianity," *Encounter* 53:2 (Spring 1992) 135–46.

4. This type of process was pointed to by Norman Perrin in *What Is Redaction Criticism?* (Philadelphia: Fortress, 1969) 39, and is used by

Asher Finkel in "The Prayer of Jesus in Matthew" in *Standing Before God*, Asher Finkel and Lawrence Frizzell, eds. (New York: KTAV Publishing, 1981) 131–69.

5. Finkel, *Standing Before God*, 131.

6. For a discussion of the use of this criteria in the context of biblical studies, see John P. Meier, *The Marginal Jew* (New York: Doubleday, 1991) 167–95.

7. Meier, *The Marginal Jew*, 176–7.

8. The Criteria of Non-projection is known in biblical studies as the "criteria of discontinuity" (or dissimilarity, originality or dual irreducibility). This would also include the criteria of contradiction and rejection. In these criteria there are indications of non-acceptance by others which would give some support to non-projection. Meier, 169–74, 177.

9. Meier, *The Marginal Jew*, 174–5.

10. Other studies include Charles Morris Addison, Stephen T. Katz, Francis Younghusband, Rudolf Otto, Adolphe Tanquerey, and Richard Woods, et al.

11. Evelyn Underhill, *Mysticism* (New York: Dutton, 1961) 80–1, 176–9.

12. Marghantia Laski, *Ecstasy in Secular and Religious Experience* (Los Angeles: Tarcher, 1961) 5–8, 37–46, 369–74.

13. Evelyn Underhill, *Mysticism*, 169–75.

14. Ewert H. Cousins, "Models and the Future of Theology," *Continuum* (Winter-Spring, 1969) 82–3. For a further discussion of this understanding, see Robert C. Forman, "Mystical Knowledge: Knowledge by Identity," *Journal of the American Academy of Religion* 61:4 (Winter 1993) 705–38. Ewert H. Cousins, *Christ in the 21st Century* (Rockport, Mass.: Element, 1992) 41–72.

15. For a review of the history of psychology and religion and the debate over the boundaries between psychology and religious/pastoral counseling, see David G. Benner, *Psychotherapy and the Spiritual Quest* (Grand Rapids: Baker, 1988) 11–52.

16. Over the fifteen years it appears that three positions have developed. The first holds that a distinct line demarcates the two fields; the second is that of two hostile camps [see William Kirk Kilpatrick, *Psychological Seduction* (New York: Nelson, 1983) 71], and the third is that of integration. [Kirk E. Farnsworth, *Wholehearted Integration: Harmonizing Psychology and Christianity through Word and Deed* (Grand Rapids: Baker, 1985)].

17. See E. F. O'Doherty, *Religion and Psychology* (New York: Alba House, 1978) 33–7. In addition to the discussion between the two fields,

there are internal debates within each of them. See Benner, *Psychotherapy,* 50–1; Janet Ruffing, "Psychology as a Resource for Christian Spirituality" *Horizons* 17:1 (Spring 1990) 47–59. This debate is important for it addresses the relationship between the fields of psychotherapy, pastoral counseling, and spiritual direction or healing neuroses, fostering integration and debate on the pathological areas of psychology and theology. The fact that these discussions are taking place points to the importance of the emergence of spirituality in disciplines in addition to systematic theology.

18. Doing a psychoanalytical study of the individual's mental and nervous disorders, especially someone who is not in the room with you, is very difficult. See Sigmund Freud, *Introductory Lectures on Psychoanalysis* James Strachey, trans. (New York: Norton, 1966) 15; James Drever, *The Penguin Dictionary of Psychology,* Revised by Harvey Wallerstein (New York: Penguin, 1952, 1964) 230. In the case of the *late* Father Price it would be extremely difficult. Such a study would focus on the psychological review of problems (we are told that we *all* have problems) and not the results of the individual's life journey. Therefore, even if it were possible to do a psychoanalytic study in the clinical sense, it would not be desirable, for the objective of this study is self-integration, but we are looking for transcendence.

19. Viktor E. Frankl, *Man's Search for Meaning* (New York: Simon & Schuster, 1963) 175–7.

20. John Welwoods, ed., *The Meeting of the Ways* (New York: Schocken, 1979) 21.

21. Abraham Maslow, "Religion and Peak Experience," *Psyche and Spirit,* John J. Heaney, ed. (New York: Paulist, 1973) 97–107.

22. Liliane Frey-Rohn, *From Freud and Jung* (New York: Dell, 1974) xi.

23. C. G. Jung, *Psychological Types* (Princeton, N.J.: Princeton, 1971) 442–7, 451.

24. C. G. Jung, *Psyche and Symbol* (Garden City, N.Y.: Doubleday, 1958) 6–9.

25. M. Ester Harding, *The 'I' and the 'Not I'* (Princeton, N.J.: Princeton, 1963) 222–3.

26. Ewert H. Cousins, *Bonaventure and the Coincidence of Opposites* (Chicago: Franciscan Herald, 1978) 18–21.

27. C. G. Jung, *Psychological Types,* 460 and *Psyche and Symbol* 22–5.

28. Viktor E. Frankl, *Man's Search for Meaning,* 175–7.

Appendix B

The Sources

The first concern in a study of this type is "does there exist enough material in both the expressive and experiential areas to construct the theologies." Fortunately in Fred Price's case there is an abundant amount of material. However, it is not systematically presented. In this case composition criticism is helpful for it helps us identify the author's motivation and objective, the audience for whom the work was intended, the various literary genre, the sources used, and the structures within the text(s). Sources in this case study fall into four categories: those written about Fred Price, those written by him, the material he edited, and the items he read or studied.

Writings About Fred Price

Even though he is the lesser-known founder of Maryknoll, we are fortunate to have three biographies of Fred Price,* a chapter or two on him in the histories of the Society,[1] Sheridan's book about the co-founders, and mentions of him in a book about other Maryknollers. There are also brief, but important, references concerning Price in the memoirs of Cardinals Gibbons and O'Connell.

In addition, there was a symposium about Price held in 1956. The results of this meeting was a collection of documents containing testimonies by people who knew him and miscella-

---

*The first biography was published in 1923 and an unpublished manuscript was completed in 1943 by George C. Powers, M.M.. It was used in the development of the most famous biography *Tarheel Apostle* by John C. Murrett, M.M. (1944).

neous pieces of data not found in any other works. Fr. Robert Sheridan, M.M., updated the symposium documentation in 1981 and printed the expanded document in a limited edition.[2] To date there has not been any attempt to construct either Fred Price's systematic or experiential theologies.

Price's Writings

There are four basic areas of Fred Price's writings that have survived: his letters to the Blessed Mother now called the *Diary*, his letters to others, of which relatively few remain, his pamphlets and articles on mission and student retreat notes, and the articles he wrote for *Truth* and the introduction to the books on Bernadette.

Father Price's *Diary*, as Maryknollers have come to call the "thirty-four notebooks," is a collection of daily letters that Fred Price wrote to the Blessed Mother from 1908 to his death in 1919.

The *Diary* was not discovered in Yeungkong, China, until 1925–1929 or for at least six years after Fred Price's death. Fr. James Edward Walsh, who found the *Diary*, was one of the first Maryknoll priests and had accompanied Price on the first missionary deployment to China. The notebooks have been treated by the Maryknollers with great reverence ever since.[3] However, the thirty-four notebooks were shelved in the Maryknoll archives until the 1940s when they were studied and used in the biographies. In the 1950s the transcribing of the letters was begun by Bishop Waters. Since then several people have put years of work into transcribing the letters.[4] The transcribed letters that comprise the *Diary* were carefully checked and then published in a limited series by the Maryknoll Fathers in 1980.[5]

The letters have a standardized format with a formal opening to the Blessed Mother and a formal, final "paragraph" and closing. Other items such as page headings and other notes were also used by Fred Price.

As one begins to read the *Diary's* letters, the early letters seem very negative. They often contain his loneliness and deepest fears but seldom mention his daily joys as reported by so many who knew him. This is not unusual with people on a spiritual searching. A search that was going on at the depth of his being.[6]

The *Diary* shows Fred Price's growing relationship with the Blessed Mother and Bernadette. He used the *Diary* to discuss his spirituality with the Blessed Mother, to describe his spiritual goals, to share his personal orientation towards the work he was doing, and to outline spiritual practices. Also he would ask for her blessing on the work and help with his sinfulness.

In addition to the spiritual letters in the *Diary*, secular letters are also available. On two occasions Fred Price's letters and personal papers were burned—once in October 1905 when the priests' residence, mission center, and "seminary" (the Regina Apostolorum) was burned down; then again all his correspondence was destroyed when Fred Price purposely burned it in 1917 (all, that is, *except* the *Diary*). Since his death the personal and business letters of Fred Price have been collected in a 1981 volume called *Collected Letters of Thomas Frederick Price, M.M., 1883–1919.*[7] His letters to Maryknoll from China has already been published in a work entitled *Maryknoll Mission Letters–China.*[8] Fred Price's letters are still being found. Recently some were discovered in Nevers, France, and South Bend, Indiana.

Other items of interest are his conference papers,[9] a small pamphlet on missiology, and a collection of retreat notes which consist of topics with a few sentences of explanation.[10]

Price's Editing

Fred Price edited two magazines and two books on Bernadette. *Orphan Boy* magazine was established in 1900 to support the orphanage at Nazareth, North Carolina. The early issues he edited are not available. The other magazine *(Truth)* was first published in April 1897.

Truth was intended for the non-Catholic families of North Carolina. The first issue states the reason for the magazine's existence:

> This little magazine is unique in its purpose, and, as far as we know, is the first venture of its kind. A Catholic periodical, it is intended principally for circulation amongst non-Catholics. Its chief purpose is to expose to non-Catholics the truth about the Catholic Church, and to correct erroneous impressions concerning it.[11]

The desire of American Catholics to explain their belief to the Protestant Americans was part of the Church's landscape since the middle of the 1800s.[12] In the overwhelmingly Protestant South this need continued into the 1900s and *Truth* addressed that need.

Circulation is estimated to have climbed to over 5,000.[13] *Truth* carried articles on Catholic theology, planting crops, and political events in the Tarheel state and throughout the world. The theological articles reflected the concerns of Protestants about Roman Catholicism in the Old North State.[14] These writings caused a sharp reaction in the Protestant oriented press[15] and enjoyed a popularity among Catholics.

While trying to reflect Church teaching, *Truth* was also the public theological proclamation of Fred Price. His own understanding shines through, in the Question Box, little quotes and sayings used as filler texts, and occasional articles that can be directly credited to him.

Certainly the courage to publish openly his understanding of events and theological positions is a credit to the editor. Since *Truth* was written at the catechism level and directed towards non-Catholics, the retention of the magazine at the public library or university level was minimal.

The following is the criteria for using articles from *Truth*. Most of the authors of the articles and notes in *Truth* can be identified by a by-line. Articles with the by-line "The Editor," "Thomas Price" (or variations thereof), or M. B. (initials taken by Fred) are considered to be Fred Price's writings. In addition, the "Question Box" of the magazine if not always written by him was published under his signature, and we will assume that the replies expressed his personal views. Also several "specially requested" articles and articles that are "emphasized" or "reused" in *Truth* are also considered as an expression of Fred's understanding.

Fred Price edited two books with lengthy introductions that he signed "M. B." The first, *Bernadette of Lourdes,* was published in 1914. He then published a smaller volume called *The Lily of Mary: Bernadette of Lourdes* in 1919. Both books give us an in-depth view of Bernadette that was accepted and fostered by Fred Price.

Important Readings

ACADEMIC TEXTS

Throughout his life Fred Price was exposed to academic texts, spiritual writings, and prayer books. Some of these he believed to be important.

Fred Price attended the Maryland Sulpician schools of St. Charles College in Ellicott City northwest of Baltimore and St. Mary's Seminary in Baltimore just before the blossoming of the theological faculty. He graduated in 1886 the year before the great writer of theological manuals Alophie Tanquerey arrived at St. Mary's.[16] Therefore, Fred Price was educated under the old Catechism method of study at both of these schools.

The college and seminary provided an excellent traditional classical college education.[17] However, there was *not* an over-abundance of theological education. Religious instruction in dogmatic and moral theology was from the popular catechisms of the time,[18] specifically the Collot and Deharbe catechisms.[19] Later Fred used parts of these catechisms as articles in *Truth* on many occasions. These texts, especially Deharbe, support Fred Price's expressional theology.

Later at Nazareth, in addition to the catechisms, Fred stocked the Regina Apostolorum mission training center for the North Carolina apostolate with a variety of manuals of theology. How many of these manuals Fred Price appropriated is unclear. Part of his daily discipline included an equal amount of time "reviewing Moral Theology or Rubrics," and doing "Spiritual Reading."[20] According to references in the *Diary* and recollections from Maryknoll students, the spiritual readings, rather than moral tomes, captured Fred Price's attention.

PERSONAL READINGS

To identify the works that Fred Price thought important, the following three criteria are used:

Extensive Quoting: Works of a theological and spiritual nature were often used in *Truth*. Only those works referenced or quoted on numerous occasions or "broken-up" and used as short articles again and again in *Truth* Magazine are accepted as having special theological importance to Fred Price.

Serious Reflection: Works upon which serious reflection or comment appears in the *Diary* or other letters.

Particular Reference: Works that are specifically mentioned by others as being very important to Fred Price or recommended by him to students at Maryknoll for spiritual reading.

Books by several authors meet more than one of the criteria listed above. They are the books by William Faber and Alphonsus Rodriguez, the Ignatian Exercises, *The Little Office of the Blessed Virgin Mary*.[21]

The Rev. Frederick William Faber's works were recommended to Fred during spiritual direction by Father Hughes.[22] Fred Price in turn further recommended them to the seminarians at Maryknoll while he was their spiritual director. Faber wrote many works such as *All for Jesus, Growth in Holiness, Foot of the Cross or the Sorrow of Mary, Spiritual Conferences,* and others. The excerpts from the books entitled *Hymns* and *Poems* were often used in *Truth* and appear to be Fred Price's most common contact with Faber's writings. Another set of works often quoted in *Truth* were John Cardinal Newman's writings on faith and the Church.

In the first few years of *Truth*, Fred Price often filled a page with text with a little segment of *Imitations of Christ* or *Following Christ*. Later he explains the book's origin to a reader.[23] He also used the book for the community spiritual readings in the evenings at the Maryknoll's Venard College in Scranton, Pennsylvania, and at Maryknoll Seminary in Ossining, New York. Other fillers frequently used were the writings of Teresa of Avila and John of the Cross.

Along with the Divine Office, *The Little Office of the Blessed Virgin Mary* was recited daily. For spiritual orientation Louis de Montfort's *True Devotion to the Blessed Mother* was used by Fred. He strongly recommended it to the Maryknoll seminarians as their spiritual director.[24]

From the above we could say that Mary was the hub of Fred Price's spiritual activity, but the spokes were from Jesuit spirituality until July 1911. Fred Price strongly desired to use Jesuit spirituality as the foundation for the Apostolic Company at

Nazareth and for the Catholic Foreign Mission Society of America, Maryknoll.[25] The Jesuit method of spirituality dominated his life from the time of the early retreats at Nazareth.[26] Along with the Ignatian Exercises, the *Autobiography of Alphonsus Rodriguez,* and his works on the practice of Christian perfection were of importance in personal reading and in spiritual direction.[27]

Finally, there is a single reference in the *Diary* to Brother Lawrence's *Gathered Thoughts:* "A pamphlet I have read—Brother Lawrence's "Gathered Thoughts"—is, I am inclined to think, just suitable for me—How he insists on the presence of God and makes it the only business of life, seems to suit me wonderfully well, Mother."[28] This book may be the most important, even though there is only one reference to it.

Step 1B of our method has identified the key sources and established their relationship to this case study. The *Diary* is the main source in constructing the spiritual theology, and *Truth* along with Deharbe's catechism, are the sources for developing the dogmatic theology. These and a variety of sources available from many points of view are helpful in giving a composite picture of Fred Price's life, thought, and spiritual journey.

Notes

1. Raymond A. Lane, *The Early Days of Maryknoll* (New York: McKay, 1951); Albert J. Nevins, *The Meaning of Maryknoll* (New York: McMullen, 1954); Sergant, *All the Day Long* (New York: Longman, 1941).

2. Robert E. Sheridan, ed., "The Very Reverend Thomas Frederick Price, Co-founder of Maryknoll, A Symposium 1956 with Supplement 1981" (Private printing, Brookline, Mass.: Brothers Novitiate, 1956, 1981). It is referred as *A Symposium.*

3. The understanding that these were special is indicated in Bishop James Edward Walsh's reaction to finding them at the Maryknoll's first mission post, Yeungkong, China. "I only knew that I had come upon a treasure—more than a few papers. I bundled it and gave it to the procurature in Hong Kong to send back to Maryknoll. I thought that I had found something authentic about Father Price" (Robert E. Sheridan, ed., *A Symposium,* S 21).

4. At times a magnifying glass was needed to read these spiritual epistles. From reading the Maryknollers' discussion of the transcription

process, it seems that a sincere effort was made to insure the accuracy of the final typed product (See Robert E. Sheridan's "Introduction" to the *Diary*. Thomas Frederick Price, "Father Price's Diary," Robert E. Sheridan, ed. (Private printing, Maryknoll, N.Y.: Maryknoll Fathers, 1980). These volumes are referred to as the *Diary*.) vii.

5. Robert E. Sheridan, ed., *A Symposium*, S 19–S 24.

6. It must be remembered that these letters were wrestling with the inner or core of his spiritual existence. Owen Chadwick gives us an insight into reading a religious man's personal sharing as he discusses John Cardinal Newman's letters to his friends. The letters were a place where he could share his other moods, melancholies, and things that weighed heavily on him. Fred Price's letters were even more personal and spiritually oriented than letters to a friend. He marked them "STRICTLY PRIVATE" or "NOTE—Private" (the *Diary*, iii).

7. Thomas Frederick Price, "Collected Letters of Thomas Frederick Price, M.M., 1883–1919," Robert E. Sheridan, ed., (Private Printing, Maryknoll, N.Y.: Maryknoll Fathers, 1981). This volume is referred to as the *Collected Letters*.

8. *Maryknoll Mission Letters - China*, (N.Y.: Macmillan, 1923).

9. They include papers presented at the Winchester Conference on Missions in 1901 and the Washington Conference in 1904. In both presentations Fred Price was concerned with mission work in the South.

10. One set of these notes appears at the end of the John Murrett's biography of Fred Price, *Tarheel Apostle* (New York: Longmans, Co.) 251–90 and the other is in the symposium gatherings edited by Robert Sheridan, M.M. (Sheridan, *A Symposium*, 158–73). Both are short reflections on topics covered in the retreats.

11. Thomas Frederick Price, ed., *Truth*, 1:1 (April 1987) 1.

12. William L. Portier, "Catholic Theology in the United States, 1840–1907: Recovering a Forgotten Tradition," *Horizons* 10:2 (Fall 1993) 318–9. Portier mentions three areas of concern (1) the Church Question—responded to by explaining the "faith," (2) Catholic Americanism—the attempt to adjust to the wider American culture, and (3) Modernism. Certainly Fred Price was involved in the first and the second, Americanism, to the extent that *Truth* claimed Roman Catholicism and democracy were not contradictory, and he defended the American diocesan model of church against German Abbot-Bishop Haid (see appendix D). However, Price spoke out against Modernism in *Truth* (see chapter 7). By the time he might have become heavily involved in the discussion of Americanism or Modernism, Fred's spiritual life had made such issues moot.

13. Robert E. Sheridan, editor, *A Symposium*, 24–5.

14. The main theological issues were: Does the Roman Catholic

Church believe in the Bible? Are Roman Catholics all unthinking agents of the Pope in Rome because of papal infallibility? Which Church is the true Church? Was Martin Luther a saint? What do the various sacraments (especially penance and extreme unction) mean?

15. *Truth,* 1:6 (September 1897) 27 and 1:7 (October 1897) 29.

16. Manuals of theology were not introduced in the seminary until at least 1887 with Tanquerey's addition to the faculty. Charles G. Herbermann, *The Sulpicians in the United States* (New York: Encyclopedia Press, 1916) 320.

17. Charles G. Herbermann, *The Sulpicians,* 258–9.

18. At St. Mary's before 1886 there "existed in the seminary only a single course of dogma and one of moral theology. This meant that all the students of dogma, whether of the first or third year, followed the same course of lectures, the same being true for the students of morals" (Charles G. Herbermann, *The Sulpicians,* 319).

19. Charles G. Herbermann, *The Sulpicians,* 259.

20. *Diary,* 5.

21. Raymond A. Lane, *The Early Days of Maryknoll,* 125.

22. Robert E. Sheridan, ed., *A Symposium,* 178.

23. *Truth,* 10:11 (March 1907) 339. Father Price usually referred to the book as *Following Christ.*

24. Robert E. Sheridan, ed., *A Symposium,* 157, and Raymond A. Lane, *The Early Days of Maryknoll,* 125.

25. Albert J. Nevins, *The Meaning of Maryknoll,* 42.

26. Rev. John O'Rourke, S.J., conducted a thirty-day Ignatian retreat for the entire Apostolic Company at Nazareth August 1905 (Robert E. Sheridan, ed., *A Symposium,* 113). During a ten-day retreat given by Father Edward, O.S.B., in 1908 at Belmont Abbey, North Carolina, Fred Price recommitted himself to the Jesuit method (*Diary,* 2). In 1911, after his time in Rome, was his last Ignatian retreat (*Diary,* 537–54).

27. Albert J. Nevins, *The Meaning of Maryknoll,* 125; Robert E. Sheridan, ed., *A Symposium,* 179; *Diary,* 23–5, 29.

28. *Diary,* 197.

Appendix C

Chronology

Bernadette Soubirous		*Thomas Frederick Price*	
Born in Lourdes, France	1844		
Apparitions of the Blessed Mother	1858		
		1860	Born, Wilmington, N.C.
Joined Sisters of Nevers	1866	1872	Father's death
		1877	SS Rebecca Clyde
Died at Nevers, France	1879	1885	Mother's death
		1886	Ordination
		1897	First issue of *Truth*
		1899	Nazareth opens
		1908	Diary begins
Recognition of remains by Rome	1909	1910	Eucharistic Congress
		1911	Lourdes and Nevers
		1911	Maryknoll begins
		1912	Lourdes and Nevers
SPIRITUAL MARRIAGE	1913	1913	SPIRITUAL MARRIAGE
		1913	Lourdes and Nevers
Title "Venerable"	1913	1914 & 1915	Pilgrimages to St. Anne de Beaupré
MYSTICAL MARRIAGE TO JESUS HOSTIA	1916	1916	MYSTICAL MARRIAGE TO JESUS HOSTIA
		1917	Leads Mission band to China

		1919	Death in Hong Kong
		1919	Heart placed in the crypt chapel at the Convent of Nevers.
Beatification	1925		
Canonization	1933		
		1936	Body to Maryknoll.

Appendix D

The Tarheel and the Abbot-Bishop

The tension between the Abbot-Bishop Leo Michael Haid of Maryhelp Abbey in Belmont and the Tarheel Father Price was on many levels. Ranging from cultural to how they wanted the Church in North Carolina to look in the future.

The first problem was multi-level cultural. There was the European regionalism versus Southern regionalism, and there was monastic life versus the "secular" priesthood. Leo was of immigrant German stock, a non-North Carolinian, and Yankee who wanted German stock monks for the abbey at Belmont and supported the immigration of European Roman Catholics to North Carolina.[1] From a southerner's point of view, this was a direct assault on the culture of the South and southerners feared Roman Catholic immigration would change the society. To the southerner these Roman Church foreigners would cause the problems (rioting) in the South just as they did in the North.

Fred was very aware of being from English stock as well as being a southerner. The German and monastic cultures were different from that of the English heritage of the population and the American diocesan tradition. The gap between the Benedictine ethos and the secular priests under his rule was never bridged by the abbot with Fred Price or anyone else.[2] In Leo's biography Paschal Baumstein states openly that "the Abbot Leo was no Anglophile."[3] He was not of the American South either. Certainly the problems between the two men were beyond personal; they were German-English, European/Yankee-Southern, and monastic-secular. They had different ways of doing things, a different constituency, and a different vision.

The second problem was their vision for the future of the Church in North Carolina. When the abbot became bishop in 1891, he attempted to place the nine counties surrounding the Maryhelp Abbey "in the perpetual care of the Order of Saint Benedict."[4] This was seen by the Abbot, monks, and secular clergy as annexation of the vicariate territory to the abbey. Due to Cardinal Gibbons' intervention, Leo was only granted control for fifty years. In 1908 he tried again to split off the original nine counties plus five into an abbatial *nullius* diocese. Fred Price, as the senior active missionary and native Tarheel, led the secular clergy in their objection to such a move. They filed an objection and met with Cardinal Gibbons in Baltimore. The Benedictine land grab failed due to the efforts of Fred Price and others, such as Fr. Christopher Dennen. The secular clergies' view of the future of the Church in North Carolina was obviously very different from the Benedictines.[5]

Finally, there was the mission center at Nazareth. It was a centralized effort and community in the eastern part of the state that in some respects rivaled the Benedictine abbey in the west. Unlike the abbot's desire to create an abbatial diocese in western North Carolina, this eastern effort's objective was to create self-sustaining parishes within the normal diocesan structure. However, Leo phrased his opposition by stating that he favored a traditional ministerial approach by the secular priests serving in parishes rather than the missionary efforts proposed by Father Price.[6] Fred, when writing to Cardinal Gibbons, openly states that he believed that Leo and the Benedictines were trying to kill Nazareth (The students sent by Fred to the college at Belmont Abbey were discouraged from returning to Nazareth). Furthermore, Fred thought that the Benedictines would seize *Truth* and Nazareth if they could.[7]

There was a personality/cultural conflict in that the bishop would make a suggestion (in the German sense a strong suggestion was to be followed) but a priest with a southern, English heritage would take it or leave it as a suggestion. Surely this made Fred seem arrogant and ambitious to Leo.[8]

The conflict between the two men was inevitable and resulted in Leo not achieving his dream of an abbatial diocese and Fred leaving the diocese to work on the foreign mission project.

In Fred's leaving he lost his "place," the basis of his "honor," his Nazareth.

It was not until 1925 that the Diocese of North Carolina recognized the vision that Father Price had for North Carolina and dedicated itself to the goals of his apostolate; by that time the leadership of the diocese had been turned over to native secular clergy rather than a Benedictine abbot.[9]

Notes

1. Paschal Baumstein, O.S.B., *My Lord of Belmont* (Belmont, N.C.: Herald House, 1985) 69. Distributed by the Archives of Belmont Abbey. Baumstein's analysis is a well-researched Benedictine reading of Leo Haid's life and is definitely pro-Haidian. Even the book's title, which is very appropo, indicates the cultural and visionary differences that must be taken into account in order to understand the tension between not just Thomas Frederick Price but all the secular clergy and the abbot-bishop.

2. Baumstein, *My Lord of Belmont,* 294.

3. Baumstein, *My Lord of Belmont,* 78.

4. Baumstein, *My Lord of Belmont,* 103–8.

5. Baumstein, *My Lord of Belmont,* 256–65.

6. *Truth* 8:6 (May 1905) 234 (See the discussion of the fire and dedication of the Regina Apostolorum priest center at Nazareth).

7. T. F. Price letter to Cardinal Gibbons, October 27, 1910, *Collected Letters,* 417. Sheridan, *The Founders of Maryknoll,* 50.

8. Baumstein, *My Lord of Belmont,* 261.

9. John C. Murrett, *Tarheel,* 59, 249.

Bibliography

Abelard, Peter and Heloise, *The Letters of Abelard and Heloise,* trans. and introduction by Betty Radice. New York: Penguin, 1974.

Ackerman, Colette, and Joseph Healey, "Bonded in Mission: Reflections on Prayer and Evangelization," *Spiritual Life* 27:2 (Summer 1981) 90–104.

Ackerman, Colette, and Joseph Healey, "Bonded in Mission: Reflections on Prayer and Evangelization," [Photocopy], Original manuscript for *Spiritual Life.*

Addison, Charles Morris, *The Theory and Practice of Mysticism,* New York: Dutton, 1918.

Alighieri, Dante, *The Divine Comedy Paradise.* trans. by Dorothy L. Sayers and Barbara Reynolds. New York: Penguin, 1962.

Ambruzzi, Aloysius, *The Newman Book of Religion.* London: Coldwell, 1936.

Barry, Peter J., *A Brief History of the Missionary Work of the Maryknoll Fathers in China,* English ed. (thesis from National Taiwan University) Taipei, China: manuscript, 1977.

Baumstein, Paschal, *My Lord of Belmont,* Belmont, N.C.: Herald House (Archives of Belmont Abbey), 1985.

The Benedictine Monks of Solesmes, *Our Lady.* Boston: Daughters of Saint Paul, 1961.

Benner, David G., *Psychotherapy and the Spiritual Quest.* Grand Rapids: Baker, 1988.

Bergeron, Henri-Paul, *Brother Andrè, The Wonder Man of Mount Royal,* trans. by Real Boudreau. Montreal: St. Joseph's Oratory, rev. ed.

Bernard of Clairvaux, *Bernard of Clairvaux,* trans. by G. R. Evans, introduction by Jean LeClercq, preface by Ewert H. Cousins, Classics of Western Spirituality Series. New York: Paulist, 1987.

_____, *On the Song of Songs I,* trans. by Kilian Walsh, volume 2 of the Works of Bernard of Clairvaux. Kalamazoo: Cistercian, 1979.

Bonaventure, *The Soul's Journey into God, the Tree of Life, The Life of St. Francis,* Classics of Western Spirituality Series, trans. and introduction by Ewert Cousins, preface by Ignatius Brady, Classics of Western Spirituality Series. New York: Paulist, 1978.

Bowden, John Edward, *The Life and Letters of Frederick William Faber, D.D.* Baltimore: Murphy, 1869.

Breton, Valentine M., *Lady Poverty,* trans. by Paul J. Oligny. Chicago: Franciscan Herald, 1963.

Brother Lawrence, *The Practice of the Presence of God,* Old Tappan: Revell, 1958.

Brown, Ina Corinne, *Understanding Other Cultures,* Englewood Cliffs, N.J.: Prentice-Hall, 1963.

Brown, Raymond, et al, *The Jerome Biblical Commentaries.* Englewood Cliffs, N.J.: Prentice-Hall, 1968.

Buber, Martin, *Two Types of Faith,* New York: Macmillan, 1951.

Burton-Christe, Douglas, Keynote Address: "New Horizons in Spirituality," College Theological Society Annual Workshop, May 24, 1994.

Byrne, Patrick James, *Father Price of Maryknoll.* Maryknoll: Catholic Foreign Mission Society of America, 1923.

Capellanus, Andreas, *The Art of Courtly Love,* translated with introduction and note by John Jay Parry, New York: Norton, 1941.

Cash, W. J., *The Mind of the South.* New York: Vantage Books (Random House) 1969.

Catherine of Genoa, *Catherine of Genoa, Purgation and Purgatory, the Spiritual Dialogue,* trans. and notes by Serge Hughes, introduction by Benedict J. Groeschel, Classics of Western Spirituality Series. New York: Paulist, 1979.

Catherine of Siena, *Catherine of Siena, the Dialogue,* trans. and introduction by Suzanne Noffke, Classics of Western Spirituality Series. New York: Paulist, 1980.

The Catholic Church Extension Society of America, *The Great American Catholic Missionary Congresses.* Chicago: Hyland, 1914.

The Catholic Mission Union, *Proceedings of the Winchester Convention.* New York: Office of the Missionary, 1901.

Catholic Foreign Mission Society of America, *Maryknoll Mission Center —China.* New York: Macmillan, 1923.

_____, *Reglement de la Societe des Missions Etrangeres D'Amerique,* Approximate Date: 1915.

_____, "Mission Notes," *Truth,* 17:5 (May 1913) 37–8.

_____, "Mission Notes," *Truth,* 17:6 (June 1913) 9.

_____, "Died at the Altar," *Truth,* 17:12 (December 1912) 27.

_____, "For the Foreign Missions," *Truth*, 18:12 (December 1914) 7–8.

Chadwick, Owen, *Newman*. New York: Oxford, 1983.

Cirne-Lima, Carlos, *Personal Faith*, New York: Herder, 1965.

Clark, Thomas D., and Kirwin, Albert D., *The South Since Appomattox*, New York: Oxford, 1967.

Considine, Robert Bernard, *The Maryknoll Story*. New York: Doubleday, 1950.

Cousins, Ewert H., *Bonaventure and the Coincidence of Opposites*. Chicago: Franciscan Herald, 1978.

_____, "Models and the Future of Theology," *Continuum* (Winter-Spring, 1969).

_____, "Spirituality in Today's World," *Religion in Today's World*, ed. by Frank Whaling. Edinburgh: Clark, 1987.

_____, "Preface to the Series" [World Spirituality: An Encyclopedia of the Religious Quest], in *Christian Spirituality*, ed. by Bernard McGinn, John Meyendorff, and Jean LeClercq. New York: Crossroads, 1986.

_____, *Christ in the 21st Century*, Rockport, Mass.: Element, 1992.

Cognet, Louis, *Post-Reformation Spirituality*, trans. by P. Hepburne Scott, New York: Hawthorne, 1959.

Cunningham, Lawrence, ed., *An Anthology of Writings by and about St. Francis of Assisi*. New York: Harper, 1972.

Curran, Robert Emmett, *American Jesuit Spirituality*, New York: Paulist, 1988.

Cuthbert, *The Romanticism of St. Francis*. London: Longmans, 1915.

Dabbs, John McBride, *Haunted by God*, Richmond: John Knox, 1972.

Dayet, Joseph M., *Total Consecration to Mary*, trans. by Angeline Bouchard. Bayshore, New York: Montfort, 1956.

Deharbe, Joseph, *A Complete Cathechism of the Catholic Religion*, trans. by John Flander. New York: Schartz, 1912, 6th ed.

DeLigny, Francis, Abbè Orsini, and John G. Shea, *Catholic Gems*. New York: Office of Catholic Publications, 1887.

Delmage, Lewis, trans. and ed., *The Spiritual Exercises of St. Ignatius of Loyola*. New York: St. Paul, 1978.

Dessain, Charles Stephen, *John Henry Newman*. London: Nelson, 1966.

Donovan, John F., *The Pagoda and the Cross, The Life of Bishop Ford of Maryknoll*. New York: Scribner's, 1967.

Dries, Angelyn, "The Whole Way into the Wilderness:" The Foreign Mission Impulse of the American Catholic Church, 1893–1925, dissertation, Berkeley: Graduate Theological Union, 1990.

Drever, James, *The Penguin Dictionary of Psychology*, Revised by Harvey Wallerstein. New York: Penguin, 1952, 1964.

Eaton, Vincent M., *American Necrology of the Society of Saint Sulpice,* Baltimore: Sulpician Archives, 1983.

Edinger, Edward F., *Ego and Archetype.* New York: Penguin, 1972.

Erikson, Joan Monat, *St. Francis and His Four Ladies.* New York: Norton, 1970.

Faber, Frederick William, *All for Jesus.* Baltimore: Murphy, 1854.

_____, *Spiritual Conferences.* Baltimore: Murphy, 1858.

_____, *Notes on Doctrinal and Spiritual Subjects.* Baltimore: Murphy, 1866.

_____, *Poems.* Baltimore: Murphy, 1857.

_____, *Hymns.* Baltimore: Murphy, 1880. (Previous London eds.: 1849 and 1861).

Farnsworth, Kirk E., *Wholehearted Integration: Harmonizing Psychology and Christianity through Word and Deed.* Grand Rapids: Baker, 1985.

Finkel, Asher, "The Prayer of Jesus in Matthew," in *Standing Before God,* Asher Finkel and Lawrence Frizzell, ed., New York: KTAV Publishing, 1981.

Forman, Robert C., "Mystical Knowledge: Knowledge by Identity," *Journal of the American Academy of Religion* 61:4 (Winter 1993) 705–38.

Fortini, Arnaldo, *Francis of Assisi,* trans. by Helen Moak, New York: Crossroad, 1981.

Francis of Assisi and Clare of Assisi, *Francis and Clare, The Complete Works,* trans. and introduction by Regis J. Armstrong and Ignatius Brady, preface by John Vaughn, Classics of Western Spirituality Series. New York: Paulist, 1982.

Frankl, Viktor E., *Man's Search for Meaning,* trans. by Ilse Lasch, preface by Gordan W. Allport. New York: Simon & Schuster, 1963.

_____, *The Unconscious God.* New York: Washington Square, 1975.

Freud, Sigmund, *Introductory Lectures on Psychoanalysis,* trans. by James Strachey. New York: Norton, 1966.

_____, *Civilization and Its Discontents,* trans. by James Strachey. New York: Norton, 1961.

Frey-Rohn, Liliane, *From Freud to Jung.* New York: Dell, 1974.

Grantham, Dewey W. Jr., ed., *The South and the Sectional Image,* New York: Harper & Row, 1967.

Grelot, Pierre, *Man and Wife in Scripture.* New York: Herder, 1964.

Guilday, Peter, *A History of the Councils of Baltimore 1791-1884,* New York: Arno Press and The New York Times, 1969.

Habig, Marion, ed., *St. Francis of Assisi: Writings and Early Biographies, English Omnibus of the Sources for the Life of St. Francis,* trans. by Ralph

Brown, Benen Fahy, Placid Hermann, Paul Oligny, Nesta de Robeck, Leo Sherely-Price, John R. H. Moorman, Introductions by Domien Vorreux, Placid Hermann, Theophile Desbonnets, Raphael Brown, Research Bibliography by R. Brown. Chicago: Franciscan Herald, 1973.

Haid, Leo to J. Fieri, undated endorsement to December 7, 1906 letter, Society of the Propagation of the Faith Materials, MPFP 2003, University of Notre Dame Archives, South Bend, Indiana.

Hanson, Bradley, ed., *Modern Christian Spirituality,* Atlanta: Scholars, 1990.

_____, "Theological Approaches to Spirituality, A Lutheran Perspective," *Christian Spirituality Bulletin* 2.1 (Spring 1994) 6–8.

Harding, M. Ester, *The 'I' and the 'Not I'.* Princeton, N.J.: Princeton, 1963.

Heaney, John J., ed., *Psyche and Spirit.* New York: Paulist, 1973.

Herbermann, Charles G., *The Sulpicians in the United States.* New York: Encyclopedia Press, 1916.

Herbermann, Charles G., et al, ed., *Catholic Encyclopedia.* New York: Encyclopedia Press, 1910. S.v. "Contemplation" by Aug. Poulain.

_____, *The Catholic Encyclopedia.* New York: Encyclopedia Press, 1909. S.v. "Eucharist" by J. Pohle.

_____, *Catholic Encyclopedia.* New York: Encyclopedia Press, 1910. S.v. "Little Office of Our Lady" by Lesie A. St. L. Toke.

_____, *Catholic Encyclopedia.* New York: Encyclopedia Press, 1910. S.v. "Marriage, Mystical" by Aug. Poulain.

_____, *Catholic Encyclopedia.* New York: Encyclopedia Press, 1911. S.v. "North Carolina," by Robert M. Douglas.

_____, *The Catholic Encyclopedia Supplement 1.* New York: Encyclopedia Press, 1915. S.v. "North Carolina."

_____, *Catholic Encyclopedia.* New York: Encyclopedia Press, 1911, S.v. "Prayer" by John F. Wynne.

_____, *Catholic Encyclopedia.* New York: Encyclopedia Press, 1912, S.v. "Soul" by Michael Maher and Joseph Boland.

Ignatius of Loyola, *The Spiritual Exercises of St. Ignatius of Loyola,* trans. by Lewis Delmage. Boston: Daughters of St. Paul, 1978.

James, William, *The Varieties of Religious Experience,* introduction by Reinhold Niebuhr. New York: Macmillan, 1961.

Jones, Cheslyn, Wainwright, Geoffrey, Yarnold, Edward, eds., *The Study of Spirituality,* New York: Oxford, 1986.

Jung, Carl G., *Four Archetypes.* Princeton, N.J.: Princeton, 1959.

_____, *Psyche and Symbol*, trans. by Cary Baynes and F.C.R. Hull, ed. by Violet S. de Laszlo. Garden City, New York: Doubleday, 1958.

_____, *Psychological Types*, trans. by H. G. Baynes, rev. by F. C. Hull. Princeton, N.J.: Princeton, 1976.

Jung, Carl G., M.-L. von Franz, Joseph L. Henderson, Jolande Jacobi, Aniela Jaffe, *Man and His Symbols*. New York: Dell, 1964.

Kauffman, Christopher, *Tradition and Transformation in Catholic Culture*, New York: Macmillan, 1988.

Kerrison, Raymond, *Bishop Walsh of Maryknoll*, New York: Putman's, 1962.

Kilpatrick, William Kirk, *Psychological Seduction*. New York: Nelson, 1983.

Kittler, Glenn D., *The Maryknoll Fathers*. New York: World, 1961.

Kosnik, Anthony, ed., *Human Sexuality*. Garden City, New York: Doubleday, 1979.

Lane, Raymond A., *The Early Days of Maryknoll*. New York: McKay, 1951.

_____, *Stone in the King's Highway*, New York: McMullen, 1953.

Laski, Marghanita, *Ecstasy*, Los Angeles: Tracher, 1961.

Lawrence, Brother of the Resurrection, *The Practice of the Presence of God*, trans. by Donald Attwater, introduction by Dorothy Day. Springfield, Ill.: Templegate, 1974.

LeClercq, Jean, *Monks and Love in Twelfth-Century France*. New York: Oxford, 1979.

_____, *Monks on Marriage, A Twelfth-Century View*. New York: Seabury, 1982.

_____, "Spiritualitas," *Studi Medievali* (3, 1962).

LeClercq, Jean, Francis Vandenbrouche and Louis Bouyer, *The Spirituality of the Middle Ages*. New York: Desclée, 1968.

The Little Office of the Blessed Virgin Mary. Chicago: Franciscan Herald, 9th printing 1979.

Luria, Keith, "The Counter-Reformation and Popular Spirituality" *Christian Spirituality, Post-Reformation and Modern*, Don Salieri, Louis Dulpre, and John Meyendorff, eds., vol. 17 of World Spirituality, An Encyclopedic History of the Religious Quest. New York: Crossroads, 1989.

Maryknoll Mission Letters - China, vol. 1. New York: Macmillan, 1923.

Maslow, Abraham H., *Religious, Values, and Peak-Experiences* New York: Penguin, 1964.

Mathews, Donald G., *Religion in the Old South*, Chicago: University of Chicago, 1977.

McGinn, Bernard, "The Letter and the Spirit: Spirituality as an Academic Discipline," *Christian Spirituality Bulletin* 1:2 (Fall 1993) 1–10.

Meier, John, *A Marginal Jew*, New York: Doubleday, 1991.

The Method of St. Sulpice. London: Griffith Farran, 1896.

Miller, Randall M., and Wakelyn, Jon L., eds., *Catholics in the Old South*, Macon, Ga.: Mercer, 1983.

Montfort, Louis Mary de, *True Devotion to the Blessed Virgin Mary*, trans. and introduction by F. W. Faber (1862), preface by William O'Connell. Bay Shore, New York: Montfort Fathers, 1941.

Murrett, John C., *Tarheel Apostle, Thomas Frederick Price, Co-founder of Maryknoll.* New York: Longmans, 1944.

_____, *The Story of Father Price.* New York: McMullen, 1953.

Nelson, James B., *Embodiment.* Minneapolis: Augsburg, 1978.

Nevins, Albert J., *The Meaning of Maryknoll.* New York: McMullen, 1954.

O'Connell, William H., *Recollections of Seventy Years.* Boston: Houghton, Mifflin, 1934.

O'Doherty, E. F., *Religion and Psychology.* New York: Alba House, 1978.

Perrin Norman, *What Is Redaction Criticism?*, Philadelphia: Fortress, 1969.

Pope, Marvin H., *Song of Songs.* Garden City, N.Y.: Doubleday, 1977.

Portier, William L., "Catholic Theology in the United States, 1840-1907: Recovering the Forgotten Tradition," *Horizons* 10:2 (Fall 1993) 317–33.

Powers, George C., *The Maryknoll Movement*, New York: Catholic Foreign Mission Society of America, 1926, 3rd revised ed., 1940.

_____, (untitled biography of Father Price) unpublished manuscript, 1943.

Price, Thomas Frederick, ed., *Bernadette of Lourdes*, J. H. Gregory, trans. New York: Devin-Adair, 1914.

_____, *Collected Letters of Thomas Frederick Price, M.M., 1883-1919*, Robert E. Sheridan, ed. (Private printing, Maryknoll, N.Y.: Maryknoll Fathers, 1981).

_____, *Father Price's Diary*, Robert E. Seridan, ed. (Private printing, Maryknoll, N.Y.: Maryknoll Fathers, 1981).

_____, "Important Notice," *Truth*, 16:1 (January 1912). New York: International Catholic Truth Society.

_____, ed., *The Lily of Mary: Bernadette of Lourdes*, New York: Bureau of the Immaculate Conception, 1918.

_____, *Missions a Duty.* Hong Kong: Paris Foreign Mission Press, 1919.

_____, "Mission Notes," *Truth*, 16:1 (January 1912): 21–2, 16:3 (March

1912): 4, 16:4 (April 1912): 45, 16:6 (June 1912): 37–8, 16:7 (July 1912): 37, 16:8 (August 1912): 31–2, 16:9 (September 1912): 33–4, 16:10 (October 1912): 40–1. New York: International Catholic Truth Society.

____, *Mission Training.* Typed booklet. Maryknoll Archives, Maryknoll, N.Y.

____, Nazareth, N.C., to J. Fieri, New York, N.Y., December 7, 1908, Society of the Propagation of the Faith Papers, MPTP 2001, University of Notre Dame Archives, South Bend, Ind.

____, ed., *Truth*, 1:1 (April 1897) through 4:5 (August 1900), Raleigh, N.C.

____, ed., *Truth*, 4:6 (September 1900) through 5:9 (December 1901), 10:1 (May 1906), 10:6 (October 1906) through 11:10 (February 1908), 12:11 (January 1909) through 15:5 (May 1911), 15:7 (July 1911), 15:12 (December 1911), Nazareth (near Raleigh) N.C.

Principe, Walter, "Towards Defining Spirituality," *Sciences Religieuses/ Studies in Religion* (12:2, 1985).

____, "Broading the Focus: Context as Corrective Lens in Reading Historical Works in Spirituality," *Christian Spirituality Bulletin* 2.1 (Spring 1994) 1, 3–5.

Rathschmidt, John, "Caste Love in Early Franciscan Literature, Especially the Sacrum commercium." Ph.D. dissertation, Forham University, 1987.

Ribet, M. J., *La Mystique Divine.* Paris: Libairie Ch. Poussielque, 1895.

Rodriquez, Alphonus, *St. Alphonus Rodriquez: Autobiography,* trans. by Williams Yeomans New York: Herder, 1964.

____, *The Practice of Perfection and Christian Virtues.* Dublin: Duffy, 1914.

Rubin, Louis D. Jr and Jacobs, Robert D., *Southern Renascence,* Baltimore: Hopkins, 1953.

Sargent, Daniel, *All the Day Long.* New York: Longmans, 1941.

Schneiders, Sandra M. "Theology and Spirituality: Strangers, Rivals, or Partners?" *Horizons* (13:2, 1955).

____, "Spirituality as an Academic Discipline," *Christian Spirituality Bulletin* 1:2 (Fall 1993) 10–15.

____, "A Hermeneutical Approach to the Study of Christian Spirituality," *Christian Spirituality Bulletin* 2.1 (Spring 1994) 9–14.

Shear, Jonathan, "On Mystical Experiences as Support for the Perennial Philosophy," *Journal of the American Academy of Religion* (62:2, Summer 1994) 319–42.

Sheridan, Robert E., *The Founders of Maryknoll.* Maryknoll, N.Y.: Catholic Foreign Mission Society of America, 1981.

Sheridan, Robert E., ed., "The Very Reverend Thomas Frederick Price, Co-founder of Maryknoll, A Symposium 1956 with Supplement 1981" (Private printing, Brookline, Mass.: Brothers Novitiate, 1956, 1981).

Slate, C. Philip, "The Culture Concept and Hermeneutics: Quest to Identify the Permanent in Early Christianity," *Encounter* Spring 92 (53:2) 135–46.

Smith, John Holland, *Francis of Assisi*. New York: Scribner's, 1972.

Sobrino, Jon, *Christology at the Crossroads*. Maryknoll: Orbis, 1976.

Society of the Propagation of the Faith Paris Material, Reference Code MPFP: 2001–2003, University of Notre Dame Archives, South Bend, Ind.

The Spiritual Legacy of the Co-founders. Unknown.

Sticco, Maria, *The Peace of Saint Francis*. New York: Hawthorn, 1962.

Tabb, William K., ed., *Churches in Struggle*. New York: Monthly Review Press, 1986.

Tanquerrey, Adolphe, *The Spiritual Life, A Treatise on Ascetical and Mystical Theology*, trans. by Herman Branderis, 2nd ed., Tournai: Desclée, 1930.

Thomas á Kempis, *Imitation of Christ*, trans. by Louis F. Hartman. New York: Crawley, 1964.

Thomas of Celano, *The Life of Saint Clare*, Paschal Robinson, trans. and ed. Philadelphia: Dolphin, 1910.

_____, *St. Francis of Assisi*, trans. and introduction by Placid Hermann. Chicago: Franciscan Herald, 1933.

_____, *St. Francis of Assisi*, trans. by Placid Hermann. Chicago: Franciscan Herald, 1963.

Trible, Phyllis, *God and the Rhetoric of Sexuality*. Philadelphia: Fortress, 1978.

Underhill, Evelyn, *Mysticism*. New York: Dutton, 1961.

Vawter, Bruce, *On Genesis: a New Reading*. Garden City, N.Y.: Doubleday, 1977.

Valency, Maurice, *In Praise of Love*, New York: Macmillan, 1958.

Walsh, James E., ed., *Maryknoll Spiritual Directory*, New York: Field Afar Press, 1947.

The Washington Conference. Washington: Washington Mission Union, 1906.

Welwoods, John, ed., *The Meeting of the Ways*. New York: Schocken, 1979.

White, John, ed., *The Highest State of Consciousness*. Garden City, N.Y.: Doubleday, 1972.

Will, Allen, *Life of Cardinal Gibbons, Archbishop of Baltimore.* New York: Dutton, 1922.

Woods, Richard, ed., *Understanding Mysticism.* Garden City, N.Y.: Doubleday, 1980.

Wyatt-Brown, Bertram, *Honor and Violence in the Old South,* New York: Oxford, 1986.

_____, *Southern Honor: Ethics and Behavior in the Old South,* New York: Oxford, 1982.

Younghusband, Francis, *Modern Mystics,* London: Murray, 1935.

Index

Sister of Charity and Christian
    Instruction, 1, 70
Society of Jesus, 139n. *See*
    Ignatian Exercises; O'Rourke,
    Edward
Soubirous, Bernadette, 1–2, 8, 16,
    28, 61–62, 66–70, 72–73,
    75–76, 79, 111–113, 127–128,
    130, 157–158
    biographies of, 151
    and Eucharist, 70
    marriage to Price, 1, 79,
        81–104, 123–124, 157
    theology of, 61, 100–103
Sources, 148–156
Spiritual Love Tradition, 13–14,
    112, 114–124, 129–130
Spirituality, 4
    criteria of judgment, 137–138,
        141–145
    as a discipline, 133, 145n. 1–2
    method in studying, 3–6,
        133–145
    mystical experience, 29, 50,
        90–92
    shock, 8
    transcendence, 110–111, 113,
        143

Sulpicians, 30–35, 37

Theology, Experiential, 100–105,
    107–110, 139–142
Theology, Expressive, 57–64,
    107–110, 139–142
Trinity, 2, 58–59, 81, 96, 100–104,
    107, 109–110
Truth, 39–41, 57, 75, 150–153,
    155n., 157

Underhill, Evelyn, 50

Visions, 24, 25n.

Walsh, James Anthony, 43–44, 51,
    54–55, 74, 76–78, 83, 97
Walsh, James Edward, 3, 78,
    154n.
Washington Conference, 43,
    155n.
Winchester Conference, 43, 155n.
Women, 62–63, 75, 84–85,
    108–109, 112–113, 124, 130
    southern, 12–13
    temptations, 84–85